D0769569

THE VAULT TO VICTORY

By Keonna Brock-Smith

©2022 KEONNA BROCK-SMITH. All Rights Reserved.

ISBN: 9798428026528

All rights reserved. No part of this book may be reproduced or transmitted in any form or by any means, mechanical or electronic, including photocopying or recording or by any information storage and retrieval system, or transmitted by email without permission except in the case of brief quotations embodied in critical reviews or articles.

Holy Bible, New Living Translation copyright © 1996, 2004, 2007 by Tyndale House Foundation. Used by permission of Tyndale House Publishers Inc., Carol Stream, IL 60188. All rights reserved. New Living, NLT, and the New Living Translation logo are registered trademarks of Tyndale House Publishers.

Scripture taken from the HOLY BIBLE, NEW INTERNATIONAL VERSION®. KJV ®. Copyright © 1973, 1978, 1984 by International Bible Society. Used by permission of Zondervan. All rights reserved worldwide.

Cover design by: K&T Graphic Designs

Edited by: Critique Editing Services

i

DEDICATION

I dedicate this book to everyone that is ashamed or just doesn't know which way to turn in life. You may have suffered through many bad breaks in life, which have caused you to believe there is no hope for you. You might believe that nothing good happens to you and never will. But I'm here to tell you nothing is impossible for God! The Lord knows our beginning, middle and end. I hope that when you read my story, growth and wisdom and the breaking of chains that had you bound will make you free in Jesus' name. Amen!

ACKNOWLEDGEMENTS

I would like to acknowledge the beautiful people who have helped me along the way. First and foremost I would like to give all the glory and honor to the Most High God for using me as a vessel as He saw fit to be able to write and share my story. Nothing is too hard for You. Through Christ all things are possible and all things work together for the good of those that love the Lord.

I would like to acknowledge the man that stepped up to the plate, Isaiah Brock-Smith. You have been a light of love, and an answer to my prayers. Despite the odds of trials and tribulations that we faced together, you stood on God's word even when I had my doubts. You made sure the assignment that God blessed me with was gonna be fulfilled. You encouraged me to keep going even when I didn't feel like it. You put in prayers to God on my behalf. Just knowing God ordained us to be, I just want to say thank you. We knew it wouldn't be easy for the both of us, but you stuck with me. You also encouraged me to continue to work on my book no matter the circumstances. You also stayed up with me many nights after our long work days and helped me edit this very book. So I appreciate you and for that I say thank you again and I love you more than you know. When God put us together I just knew I had to show my gratitude for the new love, my true love and my best friend. Know your Wourn loves you.

I next want to acknowledge my children. I have four beautiful children, three sons and one daughter. My oldest child is Damonte. My second oldest is my daughter Angel. My third child is Sean. Last but not least my youngest child for now is Adrian. I just want them to know I love them with all my heart and no matter what things look like, I will always be in their corner. I also have two in heaven who I think about as well. When I get to heaven we will be with each other again. Mommy loves you too, Deniyah and Donte (Yes, I named my unborn babies.). I also have a beautiful granddaughter named Makayla.

I also want to acknowledge a church member of mine who wrote a book before me. I really appreciate you taking the time out of your day to talk to me, to give me advice and information and for connecting me to the right people and writing a book as well. My spiritual brother Dwayne Proctor, check his book out as well:

From Prison To Pulpit. I also would like to thank Ms. Karen Rodgers who I hired as my editor. I knew she would do a great job with making sure my book is well put together, and do you know why? It's because I made sure I talked to my Father who is in heaven and He prepared the way. Amen. I would finally like to acknowledge my family and friends for the love and support they provided for my writing journey.

TABLE OF CONTENTS

CHAPTER 1
Burned

The very first thing that I can remember from my childhood is when I was six years old and I was in extreme pain. I was in the house with my two sisters, my aunt Misa, my two great-aunts, Sylvy and Mary, and my dad. I bypassed my daddy while he was sitting at the dining room table, and I headed straight to the kitchen because I was hungry. I wanted to see what he had been cooking and why it was taking so long.

My mom had taken my hair out before heading to work. I had long hair down my back, but it was everywhere because my mom wouldn't be able to redo my hair until she got off of work. I went to the stove to look in the pot and saw it was only hot dogs. I was startled because I thought I heard someone heading to the kitchen to cook. As I turned away from the stove, the flames cooking the hot dogs spread through my hair like wildfire. I can still feel the heat as I write these words. I screamed so loud that my dad ran into the kitchen. He grabbed me and wrapped a kitchen towel around my head. He didn't care whether he got burned or not, he wanted to make sure his Snup was okay, and yes, he calls me Snup based on the character from Sesame Street.

I laid on the floor shaking and crying so loud that people outside probably heard me. I was in so much pain, everything on my face was hurting and I didn't want anybody to touch me. I asked my dad, "Where is my mommy? I want Mommy!" My aunt Sylvia called an ambulance. My daddy held me, and I stayed in his arms until the ambulance came. All I could hear were the sounds from the ambulance's siren. That alone told me that I was not okay.

The ambulance attendants came in the house to get me, and when they touched me I began to scream. They pushed me past a mirror on the wall. When I looked I was covered in burns on my head and my face; my hair was gone. I was in the ambulance getting rushed to Children's Hospital Center with the sirens blasting.

My dad had called my mom and she asked him, "What happened?" My dad replied, "Snup ran into the kitchen and got burned!" All I could hear was my dad blaming himself for what happened to me because of things he had done in the past, and my mom was reassuring him it was not his fault. She told him sometimes bad things just happen.

The doctors took me to the floor in the hospital where they treated children who were burn victims. All I could do was stare at them. Some of them had burns that covered their entire bodies. I looked at the fact that I only had burns on my forehead and the crown of my head. I was thankful and I realized it could have been worse.

The doctors gave me medicine to dull the pain and scrubbed my burns. I screamed so loud that everyone on the floor could hear me cry. My dad told me that the worst part for him was hearing me scream when they had to scrub the burns. Afterwards the doctor smoothed a medicated cream on my head and forehead. It hurt so much when he touched my burns. I was in so much pain I wanted to tell the doctor to stop.

Shortly afterwards my mom made it to Children's Hospital. I spotted her and yelled, "Mommy!" She began to cry and hugged me tight. My mom started to sing to me as she rocked me in her arms. Later on that night the doctors came into my room and talked to my mom and dad and told them that I would have to undergo surgery. As a young child I was afraid because I didn't know what to expect. The doctor explained they would have to do a skin graft to start the process of healing my skin. That meant they had to take skin from another part of my body to replace the skin that had been burned. That skin would come from my butt since it had the most fat.

The next day I was so scared because of the surgery, but I knew it had to be done. The morning after the surgery the doctor said I had to stay at Children's Hospital for at least six weeks to make sure it wouldn't get infected. My mom and dad had to leave me alone a lot because they had to work and take care of my other siblings. When they came to visit they came bearing gifts for me. They knew I loved Bert, Ernie and Snuffleupagus from Sesame Street. As time went by, my skin started to heal, but scabs were forming and it looked ugly.

Packing day arrived and I was finally allowed to leave the hospital and go home. I told my mother I missed my brother and sisters and I couldn't wait to see them. I had been away from home for 6 weeks; I had never been away from home that long before.

When I got to the house my brother and sisters had weird looks on their faces. They were happy to see me but kept looking at my burns. I got to go back to school in the next couple of days. I was excited because I'd been missing my friends and I couldn't wait to see them. When I got there, I saw that they had made or purchased for me get-well-soon cards, balloons and more.

But as they stared at my face, my friends said "Ewwww, why your face look like that?" Some even called me ugly. They called me the boogie monster and other terrible things. My self-esteem fell to an all-time low And I did not want to go to school anymore.

I had been so eager to see my friends, but I had no idea they would react that way based on how I looked. I did not know a change in how a person looks could matter so much. I thought it was based on the person themself, their inward appearance that should matter most. I felt like my life was over. That was the first time I realized that the enemy knew who I was and wanted me dead. He had tried to stop me at an early age.

The Bible says in John 10:10, The enemy comes to kill, steal and destroy—but God! What I realize now looking back at the situation is that it doesn't matter what anyone else thinks about you, what really matters most is what God says about you. Romans 8:31, New Living Translation says, "What shall we say about such wonderful things as these? If God is for us, who can ever be against us?" Amen.

CHAPTER 2
The Red Truck

As I sit back and write this, God is revealing to me some of the deepest things that I suppressed for so long. When I was 14 years old my mom used to let this guy named Pete, a friend of the family, come around to visit all the time. My mom has six daughters and one son. My mom allowed him to pick us up from time to time. I guess my mom knew Pete from her childhood, it was her baby father's friend. I believe my mom trusted him, but allowing him to have a place in our lives should have been one of her red flags.

Pete seemed cool. He used to dress like a young boy, knowing he was every bit of forty, trying to be hip. I used to hate his red truck. It had very loud speakers that didn't allow you to even hear yourself think; all that bass in his truck for no reason. Every time Pete came around you knew he was pulling up, and we would respond, "Yep, Pete is here!"

I used to be excited every time he would come around. He always had snacks, and he also used to drive us around with his loud music bumping. We felt cool hanging with him, at least everybody thought we were, probably because of all that noise, and he played all of the hip songs that we knew, trying to fit into our world.

One particular day, my mom asked him to take us to my sister's house. My oldest sister Nita had moved out and had gone to live in an apartment with her dad. Pete told my mom, "Okay, I'll take them." It was my sisters Brina, Precious and I that he would be taking. We were going for the weekend, so we had to bring extra things to keep us busy, like the games each of us loved.

When Pete came to pick us up, he said, "I have to stop by my house first." I replied, "Okay." My sisters were younger than me, so I did most of the talking. By the time we got to his place it was dark outside. I don't know why it took him so long to get there, because when we left our house it was still daylight. I think he was driving in circles, killing time.

Pete had an efficiency apartment, which means he didn't have any separate rooms. Everything was in one big room out in the open; you could see his kitchen, bathroom and bedroom because there were no walls separating those rooms.

Pete told us, "Y'all will have to spend the night. I don't feel like driving; I'm tired. I will just take y'all to your sister's house in the morning." I replied, "Okay," but I was looking around his place like, *Where are we gonna sleep?* Pete already had an answer before I even got to the question; I guess he went off my facial expression. Pete replied, "I'm going to let you have the bed and I will sleep somewhere else."

Then I said, "Okay. Where are my sisters gonna sleep?" He replied, "I'll give them blankets, and they can sleep together on the floor." I was trying to figure out if I was going to sleep on the floor too because he had just said

9

I could sleep in the bed. I was confused. So I asked again, "Pete, am I sleeping on the floor with them?" He replied, "No, you can sleep in my bed, and I'll sleep over on the couch." I said, "Okay, cool!"

When it was time to go to bed, I laid in his bed listening to music while my sisters were up playing with toys. They went to sleep on the floor, and I began to doze off. I felt the bed move, and when my eyes popped open I saw it was Pete. He put his arm around my waist, but I grabbed his arm and moved it off of me. Pete put his arm back around my waist and his mouth was really close to my ear, breathing on the back of my neck.

He said, "Shhh before you wake them up! I know you not a virgin. I be seeing you and your friend with them young boys." I said, "No!" I moved his arm again. Pete grabbed me by the hand and took me to his kitchen. He put my hands on his counter and although I kept saying, "No!" Pete acted like he didn't hear me.

He pulled my pants down and my underwear, then Pete was behind me and he put his penis in my vagina. A tear fell from my eye. Next thing I knew I started dropping a bucket of tears. I was so scared. I told him it hurt as I pushed him off of me, hoping to get him to stop. All he did was move slower. I felt so dirty and disgusted; I didn't even like him in that way. My sisters were laying on the floor. I was afraid they were gonna wake up and see this man on their sister. I could not wait to get to Nita house. After he was done he went into the bathroom, but I was still in shock so I stayed glued to the kitchen counter.

Pete came out of the bathroom and laid on the couch and told me, "Go take a shower." I didn't want to move, but I didn't know what he would do if I didn't comply, and trust me I wasn't about to find out! When I went in the shower I burst out crying, holding my hand over my mouth trying not to let him hear me, so he wouldn't have a reason to come and find me.

I had to get out quickly. I was worried that my little sisters might be next. Pete said, "You know how to keep a secret, right? I know you do. Don't let this get out. I know you liked it."

Early that morning we were finally heading to my sister's house. I didn't get any sleep the night before. I was thinking, *Why me?* All night saying to myself, *It's all my fault. If only I hadn't thought he was cool to be around, maybe this wouldn't have happened. If only I was not so gullible; how could I be so stupid? Is that why he wanted my sisters on the floor? Why didn't I sneak and get a knife out of the kitchen and stab his butt up! Keonna, did you want it? You did not fight.*

The enemy was talking to me, y'all! There were a lot of thoughts running through my head and the negative thoughts wouldn't stop. At one point I wanted to kill myself for allowing it to happen to me. On the ride towards Nita's house Pete kept trying to talk to me. He kept talking to me about things I liked, like clothes and shoes. I didn't really wanna talk to him, but I answered him because I was afraid.

Once we got to my sister's house, I hurried up and got out of the truck. Pete walked us all the way up to the door, which was on the third floor – like we needed his help. He had helped enough. My sister Nita opened the door and I went straight to the back room while he chatted with her. Once he left, Nita kept asking me what was wrong. My body language had given me away. My sister knows when something is wrong with me; we are thick as thieves.

I burst out crying, and I told her he had molested me. I told Nita, "I told him no," and before I could get another word out, Pete came knocking at the door again. Nita opened the door and he had some shoes for me, trying to bribe me. I could not believe it! I had already told Nita most of what happened, so she already knew why he had bought me those shoes. I'm so happy I had opened up to her about it even though he had told me not to say anything. But I figured I never ever wanted to see him again.

My sister started yelling and cursing him out! She got on the phone and called her dad because my sister wanted him whooped. When my sister talked to my mother she had some words for her. It went like this: My sister told my mother, "Why can't your kids come to you when they need you the most? Why can't they tell you things that happen to them?"

My mom had been sexually abused when she was growing up, so she probably needed help herself, which was no help to us. My mom told my sister, "You need to get over it." I felt so disgusted, so alone; I felt like I wouldn't be able to trust another soul ever again. I thought I could trust Pete and thought he loved me like family. The whole time he just wanted to f*ck me! Plotting the whole time.

When I was telling Nita that I got molested, she talked kindly to me and told me that I wasn't molested, I was raped. I did not want to think about anything that had just happened to me or anything that I heard, so it wouldn't sink into my spirit. I was already thinking enough. I did not want any of it to register. It was very important for me to forgive Pete–not for him but for me. I did not want to hate all men, I wanted to be able to trust again. I wanted to know what real love is like, so I knew deep down inside I needed to forgive him.

The scripture says in Matthew 6:14-15, "For if you forgive other people when they sin against you, your heavenly Father will also forgive you. But if you do not forgive others their sins, your Father will not forgive your sins." If I didn't forgive him, how could God forgive me for the sins that I would commit? I'm telling you it was not easy, but it was necessary in order for me to move forward in my life without allowing the past to affect my future. Thank you, Lord, for this revaluation!

CHAPTER 3
The Transition

One of the best days of my life was when I was turning fifteen years old. I was living with my mom at the time, and she was dating a new guy named Larry. My birthday was approaching and I was starting to get excited, getting another year older is a blessing. Time to celebrate! At that time in my life I was hanging out with my best friend Dee Dee, my oldest sister Nita and my aunt Missy. We were getting ready to figure out the move for my birthday. My boyfriend Bayboo came over to see me for my birthday and he had his friends with him. He lived just around the corner.

My mother's boyfriend Larry came out of the room and pulled me to the side and started talking trash to me while Bayboo and his friends were there. Larry said to me, "You need to stop messing with these little boys. As a matter of fact, I got a nephew for you." I replied, "Bring him over, I'm not scared," and started to laugh. I was turning fifteen years old, talking like I was a grown up. Fix it, Jesus! That tells you a lot: having no guidance, doing my own thing, leaving out when I want, skipping school, just wild'n' out! I went on with my day, then three hours passed and there was knocking at the door. It was Larry again, but he was not alone. Oooh he came bearing gifts! It was three big guys. I began talking to myself, *Keonna, now you know you just turned fifteen today. Yeah I know, but I'm mature and I want the one in the middle.*

The three guys were walking towards my sister Nita, my best friend Dee Dee and my aunt Missy and me. The thoughts that I spoke in my head had manifested quickly. I told all the girls the one in the middle was mine. I was like Debo at the time, claiming whatever I wanted. It just so happened that the one in the middle came straight up to me, gave me my picture back and told me, "Happy Birthday." In my head Larry had given him a picture of me. Larry was the man, he was on point.

I started looking at what I had on; I usually didn't care. I had on some blue sweatpants, a black t-shirt and a damn skully on my head. I was a straight tomboy. I asked him his name and he said, "My name is Big C." (In my head again) "Well how are you doing, Big C?" I replied, "What name did your momma give you at birth?" He replied, "Craig." Then I said, "Well it's a pleasure to meet you, Craig!"

It was January, but it was snowing outside, and Craig wanted to take a walk with me in the snow. We walked around asking each other questions, getting to know each other and play fighting in the snow. I love me some snow. He was throwing snowballs at me and laughing. He thought everything was funny, but I got him back though.

When it started getting late, we went back to the house. I didn't want him to leave, but his friends were ready to go. They didn't make the same connection Craig and I did, so Craig had to go. Craig came back the next day and hasn't left my side since.

One day Craig called me from his house, and while he was on the phone with me, I overheard a female in the background asking him who he was on the phone with. He said, "My girl." The girl at his house said, "What do you mean your girl? You're in my house." Then they started arguing and he told me to hold on for a second. After he put the phone down all I heard was tussling like they were fighting. Honestly, at that time I was gloating and thinking, *Okay, he wants me and not her.* Thinking back I did not know at that time that was my first red flag.

Larry asked if I wanted to take a ride with him and I ended up meeting Craig's father. I was not expecting to meet his father, but it wasn't a problem for me. I'm not a shy person. I am very outgoing and boisterous. His father got in the car and Larry introduced us and said to Craig's father, "This is your son's girl. They have been talking for some time now, and she might be pregnant." All I could think was, *Wow, how rude!* I told Craig's father he shouldn't believe Larry. Craig's father shook his head and put his head down with a smirk on his face.

They finished talking and Larry and I headed back home. My mom and Larry went into my mom's room, then Larry came out of the room with his bags packed. I didn't understand what was going on. Larry came up to me, gave me a hug, and said, "I have to go, baby girl. Me and your mother don't see eye to eye." I called Craig and told him the news as I cried. I cried because Larry was the one who brought us together.

Craig said he was on his way. Later on Craig was knocking at the door and he brought gifts. There were flowers, chocolate, and a handwritten card expressing his feelings for me. We were on our way to my room, but my mother stopped us. She said, "The only person having sex in here will be me. Now go back to the living room!" I replied, "Ewww!" Craig was scared, but we went into my room after she went inside her room anyway.

We started kissing and listening to music. He said, "Hold up, I got a song for you," then he played "T-Shirt and Panties" by Adina Howard. I had never heard that particular song before, but I really love the lyrics and when we started to kiss it transitioned to something else. We got very intimate. The next day was a school day; I didn't want to go, but Craig told me I had to and said he would be waiting for me after school. That's what I'm talking about, someone who wanted to see me do good.

As time went by my body started to feel different. I was always sleeping and didn't want to do much. I went to my best friend's house to smoke and talk. I told her that my body had started to feel different. I started to get sleepy a lot and was eating more than usual. Lastly I told her I was feeling nauseous though it was rare for me to get sick. Dee Dee replied, "Girl, you might be pregnant."

My heart started pounding; I didn't think that I could be pregnant. But I thought if I was, my mom was gonna kill me. I needed to find out whether I was pregnant or not. Dee Dee decided to get a pregnancy test and we would take it to her house. We started to read the instructions on the box: one line means you are not pregnant, two lines means you are.

I went to use the bathroom, then one line appeared on the test, but so did another one. I immediately tried to blow on the stick so the line wouldn't show up! *What am I gonna do?* All I could think about was what my mom was gonna say. I started getting anxious and could not wait to tell Craig. I called and told him we needed to talk and said that I was on my way to his house. My mind started to race. *What is he gonna think? Will he want the baby? Are we moving way too fast?*

As I approached the door I started shaking. He could tell something was wrong. He took me to his room and asked me, "What's going on?" I told him I was pregnant and he said with a smile on his face, "Are you sure?" I replied, "Yes. But I have to go somewhere because I don't know what's going to happen when I tell my mother." I gave him kisses, left his house and went to my home. I was hoping I would beat my mother home. That wasn't the case, though. I thought to myself, *I'm going in my room so she won't know something's up.* I could not tell her right then, but I planned to tell her the next day. My mother was up early, so I went to the living room and said, "Ma, I'm starting to feel different in my body. I took a pregnancy test and I'm pregnant." She replied, "You better not be! Take your butt in your room. You're not having any babies in my house." My mom got on the phone with her sisters and started telling them all my business. I heard her say, "She don't know she's getting an abortion, and I'm getting the money from her dad."

I began to feel like I couldn't make my own decisions. I felt hopeless and powerless. I felt that if I said something to her she might knock my head off and there would be no more Keonna! As I sat on my bed thinking about my situation, I heard my mother coming up the steps. She opened my door and said, "You gonna get an abortion tomorrow and we gonna pick up the money from your dad in the morning." Then she slammed the door.

I immediately got on the phone with Craig. I asked him, "What do you want to do about the baby? Do you want the baby?" I was looking for a straight answer, but he told me, "I'm for whatever you want. I will back you up." That was not the answer I was looking for. It wasn't a sure yes or a sure no; I couldn't deal with indecisiveness. I cried all that night. I did not want the morning to come.

My mother was up before me. She came into my room and said, "Get ready to go. You got thirty minutes." On our way to my dad's house all I could think about was what my dad was gonna think of me. My mother pulled up to my dad's house, he gave her the money and gave me a kiss on my forehead and he told me he loved me.

As I approached the building I started to get angry. I didn't want to do it. The front desk clerk checked me in. Told me the doctor would be with me shortly. My mother was dozing off while I was freaking out. The nurse said, "Ms. Barnett, follow me." As we entered the room the nurse told me to take off my clothes and put the gown on. I looked around. All I could see was metal tools, some were sharp objects. There was a big machine with a big bright light over the bed. I thought to myself, *I hope they put me to sleep!* The doctor came into the room and told me I had to take some pills and that the nurse would be in to draw my blood. He also told me I would feel a lot of pressure and sharp pain. He said it was normal for the procedure.

My dad and mom only had enough money for the abortion, so unfortunately I had to be awake during the entire process of watching the doctor and nurse take pleasure in the murder of my unborn child. It was the worst pain ever. It felt like a big vacuum sucking the life right out of me, except not me, my baby. It was horrible! I saw the blood in the vacuum, along with the little fragments from my unborn child. I lay there in tears, saying I'm sorry, wishing it was not me on that table.

I would not speak or go outside for weeks. I did not want to be bothered with anything or anyone at all. Craig kept calling me, leaving messages saying everything was going to be ok. Eventually I answered the phone to let him know he could come see me. When we met we held each other close and cried. I knew it was time to go. I had to get free and far away from my mom. Craig and I left and went to his father's house with him and his girlfriend Rhonda. We moved into her basement; I felt like I basically ran away from home. I felt a lot better knowing I was away from my mother so I could make my own decisions.

Looking back at this I can see that I was hurting not only physically but mentally and spiritually too. I was misguided and felt alone, missing my unborn child. I felt so empty. I love my unborn child, I named him Donte. I felt in my spirit it was a boy. The scripture says, "God blesses those who mourn, for they will be comforted" (Matthew 5:4).

CHAPTER 4
On My Own

My first time leaving my mom's house to live with my boyfriend felt unreal. Months passed and we were at it again, like rabbits. Then I was getting those symptoms again. I went to get a pregnancy test. The result was I was pregnant again! I was scared because of my past experience with my mom. Making my decisions for me. I decided to tell Nita what was going on with me so someone would know.

I asked her not to tell my mother, please. I didn't want to get in trouble for getting pregnant again. I did not want my mom to take me back to the doctor's office. I didn't want to kill my baby! It was *my* decision that time so I decided not to tell her and I stayed away until I was too far along to get the procedure done just in case. When I felt my baby move for the first time I knew there was a God. As time progressed the kicks got stronger. I was so big, when the baby would put his hand or foot across my belly you could tell which one it was. The footprint was huge. I was so huge I weighed two hundred and ten pounds! I went to the doctor's office while Craig was at work to find out the sex of our unborn child. I was so excited and could not wait to surprise him. I had bought an outfit, and when he came home I told him to pull it out of the bag. It's a boy! He was so excited.

I had two more months to go. I went back home to my mother's to break the news to her. I knew she could not make me get rid of the baby now! When I got there she said, "So you really pregnant." I had only told my oldest sister Nita. I guess she had to tell. It was okay, it showed that she cared about me. My mom gave me the biggest hug and took care of me for the rest of my pregnancy. I really needed my mother's love.

My mom allowed Craig to come stay with us. My due date was approaching around Craig's birthday. The following week was Craig's birthday. I was ready to pop! On his birthday I decided to jump on him and give him the business for his birthday. All of a sudden water started to drip down my leg. I yelled, "Maaa, what's this?" "It finally happened," she replied, with a smile on her face. But I didn't have a smile. I was scared; it was all baby.

My mom rushed us to the Hospital. I was climbing the walls when I got there. I wanted to go home! Like the pain was gonna stop if I left. I was in labor for eight hours and in so much pain. I could not breathe! I told my doctor and the nurse and they said I'm fine – I ended up passing out. My baby's heart rate dropped; they rushed me out for an emergency C-Section. I woke up to a bright yellow baby boy! My mother was holding him and he was Craig's birthday present. Craig was so excited he had a son on his birthday.

I gave birth to a 9 lb 9.8 oz baby boy named Damonte. I was a teenage mom at the age of sixteen. The doctor told us we were supposed to wait six weeks to have sex. But of course Craig started to get horny and you know what men say to get what they want, "Let me just stick my head in." I told him, "Now you know we are not supposed to be having sex." But he said, "Come on, just a little bit?"

Eventually I gave in and let him get some. I told him, "You better not nut in me!" He said, "I won't!" When he was done I felt it leaking out. I asked him, "Did you cum in me?" He said, "No." I was not going for that because the evidence said otherwise. I asked Craig, "Why is cum coming out my vagina?" I ended up taking a pregnancy test and found out I was pregnant again – back living in my mother's house. I could not believe it!

I just had my baby boy, not even a whole month old, fresh out of the vagina and I was pregnant. I knew I couldn't tell my mother that I was pregnant again. I knew I didn't have the money and Craig didn't have the money for an abortion, which I didn't want to do, but I didn't want to be pregnant either. So thoughts had already started coming to my head as I was trying to figure out a way to get rid of the baby.

I tried falling down the steps. So now I'm a hypocrite because I didn't want to kill any of my children, but look at me now! I'm no better than my mom. Now I realize that she just wanted the best for me and I'm realizing that I want the best for myself too, but I know I can't do that alone. I know what I was doing was wrong, so I had to just pick up my cross. So we're having another baby!

We went out to Virginia with his dad and his girlfriend Rhonda to her house where she allowed us to stay in her basement. We stayed there for a couple of months, then I talked to my mom, and she said I could move back in with her. So I packed my stuff and I went to my mom's house and Craig said he was going to stay at Rhonda's for a little while, but then he would be coming to my mom's house soon.

I gave Craig about a week, and then I called him on the phone. I asked him, "When are you coming? My mother already said you can come. He said, "In a couple of days. Just let me finish handling something real quick." I told him he needed to come now because I had a gut feeling something wasn't right; something was about to happen. It was just in my spirit! He told me, "Okay, I'll come in two days, give me two days." I took my baby Damonte and my sister Brina and caught the bus all the way to Virginia. I went in person to tell him to bring his butt home now! Craig told me, "Stink (His nickname for me), not right now, but I can promise you I will be there tomorrow." So I left and went back home.

The next day my phone rang and the operator said, "You have a collect call from Fairfax County jail." I immediately hung the phone up and the phone rang again. The operator said, "You have a collect call from Craig." I started to cry. I was so angry. I knew my spirit was trying to tell me something and he was a hard-headed somebody that did not want to listen. I finally answered the phone and he said, "Stink, I am so sorry, Young! I wasn't trying to get you pregnant again. I didn't know what to do."

Craig ended up getting five years behind bars. I thought, *Now, what am I to do?* I'd just had Damonte and I was pregnant again. My baby was not even one yet and I was back living with my mother. I had nothing and now no one. I eventually moved in with my aunt Rhee after I gave birth to my beautiful newborn baby girl who weighed 6lbs 12oz. Her name is Angel. She was so tiny compared to my firstborn. Leaving my mother's house, I thought life would get better. Boy was I wrong.

When I got to my aunt Rhee house, I didn't really have a room to myself, I had a corner of a room. Also, I had to give her cash to stay there and the majority of my food stamps. To top it off, I still had to do everything by myself. But one day my uncle Kevin came through with his friend, Michael and his friend was trying to holla. He saw what was going on in the house every time he came over, so he offered me a place to stay in exchange for me taking care of his mom. She couldn't do things on her own and she also wore an adult diaper.

Michael was always on the go, but hey, I was living rent free, so I was with that offer! I didn't know them very well, but he seemed to be a blessing. I knew I couldn't afford to stay where I was. Michael was a great help; he used to watch the kids for me while I went to look for a job. While I went to work Michael didn't mind helping me out with my children. He was very kind and sweet. My children needed shoes and clothes.

Michael was there even if he didn't have the money. By any means necessary. He made sure my children had shoes and clothes. Sometimes he took money from his mom. I didn't agree with that, but I knew I needed it. He used to steal out of the store to get them some shoes. Like I said, by any means necessary. I really appreciated him. He made me feel like we were playing house without the rings. I used to go visit my mom and she was cool with him because she realized that he was stepping up to the plate and helping me take care of my kids. She knew he could drive, so when I had to go somewhere, she let him use the van.

Come to find out, while he was driving with the kids and me in the back seat, the police drove up behind him, and turned on their siren to pull Michael over, but he wouldn't pull over. Instead, he started speeding, and he said to me, "Keonna, I'm not going to jail." Suddenly I was in a high speed car chase with my children in the car! I was yelling, "Pull the hell over right now! My kids are in this car." He would not pull over, but Micheal was one hell of a driver. He got out of there!

I ended up liking Michael, so we started dating, but soon after I went to a mall and I met this guy named Roy. It was really getting complicated because I liked him too. He was light skinned with tattoos. I thought he was dreamy, but there was a problem. I lived with Michael and he loved my children. Why would I wanna mess that up? I told myself, I'm not here to fall in love; I already fell in love. I knew who I wanted, but I wanted to have my cake and eat it too!

I started working security at the House of Ruth and I ran into a blast from my past. His name was Tyc, and I'd had a crush on him since I was thirteen. He started popping up at my job almost every night. The problem was I was pregnant and I didn't know which one of them was my baby's father. I found out I was pregnant around three and a half months later. I was scared, and I didn't know what to say. I was so embarrassed. None of them knew about each other except Roy! How was I gonna tell Craig that I was pregnant? What if he asks who the father is, I think we're gonna have to spin the wheel!

I decided not to tell him right away. I had to plan ahead to go to the clinic because I didn't want to lose my best friend, my love. Willing to take my child's life for love. When I got to the clinic I started having second thoughts. I didn't want to kill my unborn child so when the doctor called me in the back and told me to lay on the table, I layed on that table and cried my eyes out just talking out loud speaking to God. I didnt know at the time if He was real or not but I begged that if He can hear me don't let the abortion happen. Suddenly, God answered my cry. The doctor came back into the room and told me he had good news and bad news. He asked which one I would like first. I told him, "The bad news. Might as well get that part out of the way right?" The doctor said, "The bad news is that we can not give you an abortion today because you are further along than expected. The good news is we have room on the schedule in two weeks to do the procedure but you will need to pay more money because you are far along in your pregnancy than expected." Little did the doctor know that was great news. God answered my cry in prayer. God gave me grace and this day I choose life. I still was not out of the clear just yet. I couldn't believe who I saw in the waiting room. It was the girl that went with me to see Craig; her boyfriend was locked up as well with my baby's father Craig. She asked what I was doing there. I just shook my head. She told me she was with her friend for support. I thought, *Great, now something else is on my plate.* The doctor finally called me back to the room. She ended up telling Craig that she saw me at the clinic. That's the least of my worries at this point.

I went to visit Craig in prison. I told him about the news of me being pregnant. I told him I could understand if he didn't want to be with me any more. But Craig surprised me because he still wanted me, so he proposed. I was excited, but the location he was at was Saint Brides Correctional Facility. I said yes to his proposal, but we had to wait six months. I had to drive every month to see him and do marriage counseling.

On the day of the wedding my mother and my baby girl Angel went with me to be witnesses of the wedding. As I approached the prison Craig's friends were on the yard yelling, "Congratulations! Okay, Big C! Whoo whoo!" I was smiling from ear to ear! I could not wait to see him, I knew this day would be special.

He got to hold his daughter for the first time, and we were getting married. We got to take pictures and they said we could have a room, but Craig said, "No, I'm not having sex with my wife in this place! I can wait till I come home, that will make it more special." I went home married at the age of nineteen years old.

Four months after my wedding my third child was born and I knew he was special because God allowed me to have grace. So I knew God had plans for him. I gave birth to a handsome baby boy. He weighed 8lbs 4oz and his name is Sean. Sean is my chosen child.

My children gave me a different outlook on life. Especially about how my life was about to change. I would soon be responsible for three little people, scared of not knowing what to do and if I would be a good mom. I was worried about how I was gonna take care of us financially. I had to grow up real quick! Scripture says, "Children are a gift from the Lord; They are a reward from him" (Psalm 127:3).

CHAPTER 5
God Blocked It

I was at the point where I was going through a rough patch in my life. I was living at my dad's house with my children, Damonte, Angel and Sean. Craig was still locked up, and I felt like I had to do what I had to do. I needed income, so I applied for cash assistance and food stamps. I kept worrying that they might put Craig on child support when he got out of jail. My mind was wondering about a lot of things.

Several weeks passed, then they finally gave me cash assistance. I was granted $389.00 a month; it wasn't much, but it was a start. I could at least get my children things they needed. Still, I knew I had to find something soon to bring in more money. I needed to put a plan together. I would need a babysitter and I would have to pay the babysitter. I would also have to be able to trust them with my children. It was a lot to think about. My friend at the time Steve and I decided to go out. I talked to him about what was going on and we walked around on Florida Ave. This man pulled up beside me and asked if I was working. I asked him, "Does it look like it?" I guess he asked me that question because I was on the strip where they do prostitution. I had on sweatpants, though. I wasn't really dressed in anything sexy yet. Steve and I were chatting about it. Steve said, "Look! You better take all these women's customers." I started thinking about it. I came to a conclusion and I said to Steve, "Right! I can get the money I need to take care of my children, plus. Count me in!" I told Steve, "Let's go tomorrow. I will get my dad to watch my babies."

The next day while the children were asleep, I got dressed, but I refused to dress like a hooker. I just put on some blue jeans and a shirt. My ideal plan was to have Steve be with me to make sure I was good. I would pick who I slept with to at least make sure it was to my advantage. I didn't want an old creepy-looking man on me. I wanted someone fine that I would date. If I saw him in public without selling my body, I still would have the mentality that he could get it.

When I posted on the street, it didn't take long at all for me to get a customer. Me and Steve were out there for about 5 minutes when a truck pulled up and asked for my price. I didn't even think about that until he asked what my price was. I told him $150 was the price. I told him what the deal was. "When you cum it's over; my job is done," I said. He agreed and I said to myself, *This is gonna be so easy because I have a snapper, LOL.* I was definitely right. In three minutes I got $150. I went back out thinking, *Who's next!*

Another car pulled up, but I said no to him. He wasn't my cup of tea. I didn't care how much money he had. Another car pulled up and he offered me a hundred bucks. I told him, "Sorry, that's not enough. Come back when you get the rest." That is exactly what he did. He came back in 10 minutes with the rest of the money. I told him the rules and he was down. He lasted about 5 minutes. I guess that's why they have to buy vaginas; it's because they can't hang. I was ready to call it a night. I had $300 in my pocket and it had taken less than 30 minutes.

When I was ready to go another car pulled up on us and he was fine. He had tinted windows. I told him I was about to go in the house, but he was trying to get some of me. I asked Steve what he thought. He said, "B****
you better get that money! It doesn't take you long anyway." We started laughing and I agreed. The guy wanted to go to Hamilton Park; I told Steve I would meet up with him in 15 minutes. I felt a little scared because I didn't have Steve watching over me. We ended up having sex and just like the first customer, he was done in 3 minutes. I bent down to put my shoes on and pull my pants up and I felt something pressing on the back of my head. I wasn't looking and I just grabbed whatever it was. When I turned my neck to see what it was I was in shock at the sight of a gun. I was holding the barrel and the guy pulled the trigger. I heard the click, but it didn't go off. I immediately froze.

A bright light appeared before my eyes, and I started seeing images of my children, my mom and my dad. Everybody who was connected to me flashed before me like it was coming from a projector. The guy that pulled the trigger was in shock. Looking back on it, I believe he was witnessing God at that very moment. He freaked out and took all of the money I had, including my cash assistance grant. I was shaking in disbelief.

One thing I know for sure is that there is a God, and He has so much in store for me. I'm supposed to be dead, but God blocked it. It was foolish for me to put myself in jeopardy like that. I was selling my body to people I didn't know, and it almost cost me my life. I would've lost my children, my family and my soul purpose because I was ignorant. Only God knows where my soul would've gone if that bullet had prospered against me. I believe in God's promise that even when I make my bed in hell He is still with me.

CHAPTER 6
Finding God

I was on a bumpy road, my mother decided to move to south carolina and I ended up moving with her as well. It was the worst! She treated my kids like they weren't her grandchildren. She was acting really strict and mean. She charged me for everything. For example : I had to pay my mother for tissue, food, rent, transportation and to babysit. I was at a rough patch in my life. The hills were so steep that I was ready to follow them to the edge. I felt like everyone was against me. I wanted to move out of my mom's house. I had to grow up fast by paying bills and learning to do things on my own. I had to either pay for it or work for it. Nothing was handed to me. I was trying to find a job because Bella (My sister) said if I can get a job, she could help me find a place. I didn't like my children with my mother because my mother used to yell at my children for no reason when my kids wanted to play. She wouldn't allow my kids to be children. They always had to sit down and when they moved they got yelled at or popped. Bella even recognized it and said she needed to hurry up and get me a place so I could get out of my mother's house. I strongly agreed because I didn't like someone hitting on my children, but I couldn't do anything about that because it was my mom.

I finally got a job working at Charley's Philly Cheesesteak at the mall, which was pretty cool for my first job. They hired me as a cashier and I got big tips! People liked my personality and guys were always hitting on me. One day My manager told me if I could sell 10 large sandwiches on my shifts the tips would be all mine because my job used to take the tips and split them. I was hustling by telling guys that were flirting with me they had to buy a large sandwich and leave a tip, with a smile on my face. That would get them every time.

So now that I had a job I needed a babysitter. I got the government to pay my mom $900 for watching my children. On top of that I needed a ride to work because in South Carolina you have to have a car to get where you need to go. I asked for my mom to drive me to work because I didn't have a car yet. I needed a lot of things I didn't think of until I had children, but now the pressure was on and I had to grow up really quick. Even when the government was paying my mom to watch my children, she still charged me for transportation. I guess the $900 dollars didn't include the rides.

Bella came to me one day and said she had good news for me. She got a two bedroom house for me that I could move in too right away. She also said she would help me get furniture in there. It was like prayers were getting answered, but I wasn't praying. Nothing but God, He knew I needed to get away because I was getting taken advantage of.

I was at the point where I had a house, but it's gonna cost me because I added more to my plate. My mom was still watching my children, but I had to catch a cab to drop the babies off at her house, which cost me $17 dollars to get to my mom's house every day. Then I had to catch another cab from my mom's house to work, which was another $15 dollars. These cab fares sound like good deals but while I was living in South Carolina I was getting paid minimum wage, which was $6.50 an hour. I had to pay $600 dollars a month for rent, not including utility bills.

After I was settled in my house for a while, Bella and I had a falling out, which caused us to stop talking to each other. Bella was very bossy. I was giving Bella the money to pay for my bills before we stopped talking to each other. So when we stopped talking to each other I was back to square one, giving my mother the money for my bills.

As time went past Bella and I eventually started to talk to each other again. Bella wanted to talk to me about something important though. My sister told me, "You're gonna need to sit down for this. For the past 6 months, you've been paying the bills through my mother. I got the landlord to decrease the rent by putting in a word for me. The entire time when you thought you were supposed to be paying $600 a month, you only needed to be paying $400 dollars a month." So that meant every time I gave my mother the rent money, $200 was supposed to be saved for bills. But my mother was spending the $200 dollars on herself.

I was crying when I first heard about that. But I thought to myself- *Why am I crying? Let me just go ask her because she might still have it*. But I already knew that my sister just gave me the hint that she was hoarding my money. I asked my mom about the money. She said, "What money?" I replied, "The money left over from the rent Bella said she knocked off for me." My mother said, "I've been giving you that money back when you needed your bills paid." I responded, "Every time you gave money for the utility bills I paid you back, so I was paying you for my own stuff."

My mother was acting nonchalant and acted like she didn't need to say anything else to me. I wasn't going to disrespect my mother, but I knew I had to get away from that lady! My mother was taking money from me knowing that I was struggling. It was like she wanted to see me fail. So I had to do the unthinkable to get her out of my pocket and get my children away.

There was a boy that liked me from work. His name was Terry and he was having trouble where he was living. He had a car which was good for me so I offered for him to stay with me and I could have money knocked off from getting cabs to work. A monkey wrench got thrown in my plans because when I let him stay I made it seem like he was dating me, but that wasn't the case. I just needed a ride to work and extra money to stay in my pocket.

That entire situation went south real quick. I wanted a cigarette but none of us had any more. Terry was too tired to go to the store so I took his car keys. I knew there were some hoodlums outside so I asked them which of them could drive me to the store. I couldn't drive at the time and I didn't have a license either. All the guys out there were trying to take me to the store. There was one that particularly stood out from the group. He told his friends with authority, "I GOT IT! I SAID GOT IT! The rest of his friends backed down and I got someone to drive me to the store. I asked what his name was and he told me to call him P. I got the cigarettes and came back to my place.`1 Meanwhile Terry woke up looking for me and saw me from the window when we pulled up.

I saw Terry and I said, "Oh Lord, he woke up." P asked, "You gonna be good? Do you need me to come upstairs?" I replied, "No I'm good. If he does something he's gonna wish he didn't." I went into the house and started smoking my cigarette on the bed. Then Terry came to me and said, "Oh you just gone take my car and let n*ggas drive it." I told him, "You were asleep and I didn't want to wake you up." He started yelling and cursing at me, but I went on the bed and kept smoking my cigarette in peace because that's what I went to the store for.

He climbed on top of me and pinned me down. I was yelling at him, "Get the F off of me!" Precious heard me because she was in the other room with my children. She came into my room and told him, "Get off of my sister." He turned his head for a second and I broke free, then I punched the s**t out of him. I cursed him out, went to the closet, grabbed a belt off of the rack, and walked into the room. I took the buckle and beat his butt with it to let him know don't play with me.

He was bleeding from his head then it started leaking on my carpet. He was going down the steps and while he was I kicked him down. I told Precious to call my mother to come get us because I thought I was going to jail. Thank God I didn't though. Then what Terry did next was bizarre; after all that beating, he still wanted to be with me. My mother and her husband came and told him to roll out. But when he was leaving he gave his number to my mother. She told me what he had done and said, "That boy ain't had enough.".

Afterwards we locked the house up to make sure the coast was clear and the police weren't coming to get me. I stayed with my mother after that but only for a day. The next day I went back home and I was on my own with my two kids. It was difficult to pay the bills and pay for cabs all by myself. My manager was taking me home the majority of the time because he knew the situation between my mother and I. Come to find out he was taking me home because he wanted to be my sugar daddy.

I did long nights so much that when it came to the morning I had to focus on my children eating breakfast, taking a bath and wanting everything. I couldn't really give them all my energy because I was drained from working hard. I got tired of paying my mother, so eventually I started locking my children in my room. Sean would be asleep and I would have to tell Angel and Damonte to be quiet. But Damonte, who was only 3 years old, knew how to break out the door. He broke out the door with his sister and all I heard was pitter patter around the house. I jumped to my feet looking for them thinking, *Where did they go?* How did he get out of there? I still don't know how he could do that! He ended up downstairs in the kitchen. I had twelve boxes of cereal and they emptied all the boxes and made a tower with the cereal in the middle of the floor. I not only got a house trashed, but a pile of food on the floor that my children are supposed to eat. Damonte started becoming a toil on me because he was spoiled. He cried for no reason sometimes and when he cried he made Angel and Sean cry too. Three children crying on a regular basis was making my head spin, it was always Damonte doing things in the house. From biting his sister, to throwing stuff around the house when he got mad. I'd finally had enough of him being a terrorizer in the house. I was having a mental breakdown. I didn't want to be in South Carolina anymore. I didn't really have help, and Damonte kept scrambling around the house. It got to the point where I had to lock him inside his room so I could get some sleep! That didn't work because he started banging on the door and throwing stuff at the walls. He had the neighbors banging on the walls because he was making so much noise.

I jumped out of my bed in a rage! I grabbed a belt and went to open his door and I started swinging the belt at him. I didn't care what direction it went in and then I realized I hit him with the buckle. It bruised him instantly and caused a purple bruise on his arm to be purple. I grabbed him and started crying because I felt angry inside. All I wanted was for him to be quiet. I felt I was losing it, so I hurried and grabbed some ice for his arm. I didn't tell my mom or my sister what happened because I didn't want my children to be taken away from me.

I waited for a week to go by, and then I called my best friend at the time (DB), especially since she wanted to be the godmother. I told her that I needed her to get Damonte for a while, so I could regroup.

She came and got him, and she bought him a few things while he was there in her care. Two or three days later she called me upset, telling me that Damonte had broken her playstation and messed up the clothes she'd just bought him by playing in the mud. I had no choice but to go get him a couple days later because she kept complaining. She'd only had Damonte for about 4 or 5 days, but that was enough to calm my nerves down.

There's a saying that what you dish out as a kid, you're gonna get it back in return 10 times worse when you have a kid. Now, I know that I never should've received that in my spirit. What you receive is what will manifest, especially if you believe it. The Lord said life and death is in the power of your tongue, what you speak comes to life and what you don't cast down will manifest.

I deeply regret hurting my child;things that I thought were sweet being a teen parent turned out not to be the case at all. After I got Terry out of the picture I liked the neighbor that drove me to the store, something about men that show they the boss of the group really gets me hmmmm. Pierre started to come to my house and check on me and see if I needed anything but I was the type that really didn't ask for things because people tend to remind you of that later. Pierre came to me one day early in the morning telling me I was pregnant. I'm like and how would you know before I do? He replied " I've been sleeping a lot and I started to eat, look boy I'm getting fat " And Pierre started to lift his shirt up to show his fat boy stomach. Pierre was making me nervous about what he was saying so I took a pregnancy test and I was pregnant Omg! Craig would be home in a couple of weeks. Pierre wanted me to keep the baby but I could barely understand what he was talking about with the accent that he has plus he already has a daughter. I like him but he was not ready to settle down. He also decided to tell his other baby mother that I'm pregnant like it was any of her business. She started coming around a lot. She was definitely the jealous type. I'm not about to deal with that drama. I got a phone call from prison. It was Craig who got news about his release date. He was getting released in a week. My heart started pounding. I was excited and afraid at the same time I asked Craig would they let him move to South Carolina? He said no he has to stay in DC if he leaves the state he violates his probation and back to jail he goes. That answer right there bought me some time. I asked Pierre for the money so I can get an abortion. I really didn't want to do it but it was crunch time. Time is winding down! Pierre refused because he wanted me to have his baby. Plan B, I went back to DC and got the money from my dad. I just had to hear his lecture first. I already knew where to go. All I was thinking about was Craig. I was not thinking about my unborn baby or nobody else. I wasn't even thinking about myself in the matter. At this point I've realized I'm mistake prone. This time I knew what they were gonna do so I prepared myself I tried not to look at all of the tools and machines that were around me, by the way I don't think anyone is really prepared for killing their child I had to coach myself through this in my head I said *Keonna don't look at the machines and try not to focus on the pain just do it, think a happy thought Craig is coming home and you get to start your life no more boys just you and him.* I can not believe I was at the clinic again. They were killing my baby again. I felt bad afterwards. I got that feeling I had with the first one, depression. When I'm depressed I don't want to be bothered. I would isolate myself from everything but I don't even have time to do that. I ended up staying at my dad's house for three days to allow my body to regroup. Back to South Carolina I go, Craig was supposed to be getting released in four days but the inmates had a riot at the prison which caused his release date to be pushed back. I got another phone call days later from a (240) area code. I'm like who is calling me from a 240? To my surprise it was Craig who asked me where I was. I said in the house I was blushing from ear to ear. I was tickle pink! He told me again "I can't come down there, you're supposed to already be here waiting for me." In my head I'm like *You have know idea of the sh** that I was through while you were away. I told* Craig I can't just stop, drop and roll out. I asked him if I would come where all of us were going to stay. He said, "Man, let's worry about that when you get here." I ended up leaving everything behind my house with all of my belongings. I only took my clothes and the children's things. I left my job, my family and my baby father even though I did not keep the baby. Just like that I was headed back to DC to reunite with my love. We ended up staying over Craig's aunt's house and she already had a house full. Every room had a family in them so we were deep but I really appreciated her for letting us stay with open arms. I had left my two bedroom house just to sleep on a full size bed and my husband and I slept on the floor. The things you do for love. I was just happy that he was home. There was too much going on in that house. My clothes, shoes and also money started coming up missing. It didn't make no sense. It was definitely savage mode in there. Since Craig had been back he was not the same Craig that I knew. Craig had a different agenda he became abusive with his mouth and very disrespectful. Every time he got drunk here he go, "I ain't sh** you a hoe and a slut you couldn't wait five years until I get home, you anything. You went out here and got a whole nother nigga to dick you down." I said, "Craig I thought we already talked about all of these things and you still wanted to be with me." Let's just say he was putting on a show in front of his family. Letting everybody in our business. Or should I say my business? Craig ended up cheating on me with his ex-girlfriend. He knew I didn't like her but she looks like a monkey anyway so we even. This girl knew we were together and still pursue him. She said F*** me! Everyday I was cleaning up the house because I didn't want any roaches to get in my children's ears. I had to do something, I asked myself *Keonna what are you gonna do now? You can't go back to South Carolina.*

You really didn't like it, not convenient enough to get around, and had to do things on my own. I might as well stay in DC and figure things out. My dad's here and I have family here as well but the reason I left was because I was making the wrong decisions here as well. Something have to change for the better Is this it to life you fall for someone and they treat you like sh** and you on your own? I told Craig's aunt I appreciate her for letting my entire family stay in her home but please give me thirty days and we will be gone. Sometimes you have to get fed up with situations to get you to move. When Craig got home from hanging with his friends or cheating on me I told him I'm going to a shelter. I really didn't want to go but I have to do something. I have a whole family and they are all babies. I'm not about to separate us. The shelter was actually clean and the staff was very welcoming. Craig ended up going with us and realized we had rules and had to comply. We had to be back in the shelter at 8pm unless you had a job and neither one of us had a job at the time. Craig had a problem with that so he left his family in the shelter and did his own thing. I really hated myself back then. I already had low self esteem so whoever showed me a little interest i would roll with them just for the attention or to feel love. I could not believe all of the things that I went through and sacrificed my body my life to make sure I stayed a float for this ungrateful man or should I say boy, that's treating me like sh**. Craig's out of the shelter. I'm so stressed out I'm starting to lose sleep and weight. I'm not eating right. All I do is smoke cigarettes like crazy. Guess who decided to drop back in our life after two weeks of partying. The shelter said the only way Craig would be allowed back in is if I give my consent. I really shouldn't but I was going crazy with all of them, I wasn't actually sleeping or eating so why didn't momma need a break from life? I know I had a way out and I didn't even realize red flags were everywhere.

We ended up moving out of the shelter into a transition home. It's basically an apartment with rules. We had apartment checks with no visitors but I made a friend there I loved her and her children we grew a bond that is unbreakable they are family now being around them made the days go much smoother. We looked out for each other. The whole process took about a year and some change but trust me it was worth it when you and your family can be safe and out of harm's way.

I got on the phone with my mother and told her what I was going through. Next thing I knew she was in my ear saying, "Craig is always outside chilling when are you gonna realize you need someone that's gonna help you with your children that's his damn children too". You know something she was right. I'm always in the house no matter what the father doesn't do, the mom has to at least I do. I was crying all the time just going through the motions of depression. Not having many to talk to about what was going on. My friends were doing things teenage children were supposed to do, like have fun, so they didn't really have time for me any more. I was just ready to give up! I could not take life anymore.

Craig wasn't really listening to what I had to say. All he was worried about was being on the block with his friends and family, not really making money, just loving the streets. Craig left back out and I went to the kitchen and was crying so hard I grabbed a knife. I held it to my wrist and I began to slice my arm multiple times. I fell to the floor and I felt like I was going to pass out from the blood. I didn't care anymore. I'm just tired of everything and being mistreated. Craig came back home and yelled at me, "Keonna, what did you do?"

and started to wrap my wrist up with a towel and held me tight. He told me, "I love you too much. You have a lot to live for."

Craig told my sister Nita the news and that upset her. She came over to pick me up and take me out. Nita hasn't seen me in a while. Nita saw that I had lost a lot of weight, she could tell that I was depressed. We went out for dinner and she invited her two best friends out with us and made it a girls day out. We talked about a lot that was going on with me. It felt good to just get it all out in the open. The next day Nita came back. She took me to a church with her and her best friends out in Baltimore. I have never been to this particular church before. The preacher was preaching and he just stopped and said, "Whoa, it's people in the audience that wanted to hurt themselves."

I looked at my sister and asked, "Did you tell him?" She said, "No." She'd never been to that church. I immediately broke down. The pastor asked if we could stand and follow him as the congregation began to pray. He talked to us in the back. It was four of us and he told me I have a calling on my life, and God is not done with me yet. He prayed for me, and I felt a weight lift from my shoulders. At that moment I knew there was a God. No one could have known I was trying to hurt myself but my baby daddy and my sister.

I started going back to church. I'm a believer that Jesus is real! The bible says, "Study to shew thyself approved unto God, a workman that needeth not to be ashamed, rightly dividing the word of truth" (2 Timothy 2:15). My sister Nita introduced me to a church called Life Covenant Christian Ministries. A good bible based church. The pastor was preaching a good word, and it was hitting home for me. I could even understand the message. When I used to go to other churches I really didn't understand what they were talking about and that was not good at all especially if you really want to change for the better. Everything he was preaching about was everything I was going through. I ended up joining the church. I felt at home praising God!

I started to grow in the things of God and started to pay attention when the Lord spoke to me. God told me to "Come from thy people and cleave to me." I've been obedient and have started to trust in the Lord. A shift took place in my life for the better. I used to smoke heavily, both marijuana and cigarettes. I told God I was going to quit on New Year's. Have you ever heard of a phrase that says If you want to make God laugh tell Him your plans. He told me to quit now. It was the hardest thing I've ever had to do, at least I thought it was.

The first day was a doozy. I would usually quit for the entire day until night time. I felt I was weak because I always gave in at night. My flesh was not under subjection at all. At that moment I realized I wasn't in control over my body. It was controlled once I realized it. I felt the chains break off my hands and feet! This time was different. I tossed and turned all night and I told God to take the taste out of my mouth. I told him, "God, I trust you."

The next day I chewed gum, took a walk alone and decided I'm not hanging around the same crowd I was told to separate from. I had to give myself a fighting chance. The third day Craig came home and said, "You will not believe what I found." He opened his hand and showed me a twenty dollar bag of hydro marijuana. They call it pack now. I yelled at him, "Why would you show me that!" I grabbed it from him and went to the bathroom and flushed it down the toilet. I was pissed.

I was on my third day. *Why doesn't he want what's best for me and him?*

I had to take a walk after that. I came back home and I had to use the bathroom. I lifted the seat back up; the devil is a liar! The bag had resurfaced even though I had flushed it before I left. There's a fight between good and evil. I had an encounter with both and I realized it was a test that I had passed. Glory hallelujah! Obedience is greater than sacrifice. I am free. No taste for cigarettes or marijuana. I have been clean now for nine years. I can go around people who still do it and God is in control of me. Thank you, Lord.

The scripture that means the most to me is Matthew 7:7-8, "Ask, and it shall be given unto you; seek, and ye shall find it; knock, and it shall be opened unto you: For every one that asketh receiveth and he that seeketh findeth and to him that knocketh it shall be opened." All I had to do was acknowledge it was a problem and I wanted to be free, then I had to talk to God about it and then have faith in His word knowing that He has a way out. Then I had to trust the process and pass the test along the way. Now I am free, glory to God!

"Trust in the Lord with all thine heart; and lean not unto thine own understanding. In all thy ways acknowledge him, and he shall direct thy paths." (Proverbs 3:5, 6)

CHAPTER 7
Renewing Hope

After 10 years of marriage with Craig we decided to renew our vows. I did not get to have a family at my first wedding. Our pastor said we could renew our vows at the church at no charge. My aunt Missy is my ace, we were always close. I asked if she could be my matron of honor. Aunt Missy said, "Of course, I would love to, niece!" She was smiling. You could tell she was happy for me. We went everywhere together, we got our nails, feet and hair done. Aunt Missy helped me pick out my wedding dress and all. The day of our wedding I had no family support except my aunt Missy, aunt Tracey, my big sister Nita and her baby's father. Two of (craig's cousins) were there as well.

I was so hurt, but I tried not to show it. I did not think I was important and I felt like no one liked me. There really wasn't much going on in my life at that time, Craig was always in and out of jobs. But the Lord blessed me with a job. Finally, I didn't quit or get fired within six months. The Lord used my aunt Missy to be a blessing to me and help out with the wedding because Craig didn't help at all, which was a red flag. Why was I so gullible?

The reverend from our church walked me down the aisle. All I could think about was, *Why isn't my dad here?* He had so many excuses as to why he couldn't come. I'm telling y'all he is not even handicapped or anything. He is in good health, so what really was the problem? My feelings were everywhere, but this time we had written our vows. My church family came through for us; we love them so much. We had a cookout at Craig's family house afterwards. A lot of people showed up to help us eat but weren't there for the wedding.

Time has passed, our faith has been tested with trials and tribulations. We weathered the storm through it all. From infidelity on both sides, to division in the home, always yelling and fighting. We felt ourselves getting far away from God. Every time something went wrong I could not find myself praying for the Lord to fix the situation; instead, I had a closed mouth.

The enemy kept me quiet to the point where we were not even praying for each other. The only time we prayed was if I led our family into prayer when we were in the car. Which eventually led to separation. While separated I had time to talk to God and I asked Him, "Why am I going through this?" I asked God to give me a sign of what to do and how to get to the destination He has in store for me. God showed me through one of Craig's cousins that passed away.

I showed up to pay my respects even while we were separated. I still cared for the family, they had become a part of my world. The Lord spoke and gave me a word dealing with relationships and how a man should cover his wife, and the wife should pray for her husband. The preacher talked about not giving up – the story of my life!

We immediately got back on track. My husband started changing how he did stuff, like he would help out with cleaning, we'd go out on dates a lot more at local restaurants. So by Craig showing me he could put in the work, I started submitting to my husband.

Unfortunately, it was only for a brief moment he did those things, then he went back to his regular ole self. Red flag again. It was hard to submit under someone who did me wrong so many times, but I knew my faith was not in man, it was me trusting the Lord. He knows what's best for me. Then I had an epiphany: God didn't say submit to my husband; ladies, God said submit to your husband if he is following and submitting to Christ. The red flag again. Craig was not doing that! In the Bible it says "My people are destroyed for lack of knowledge." (Hosea 4:1)

Scripture says in Ephesians 5:22-33, "Wives, submit to your husbands as to the Lord. For the husband is the head of the wife as Christ is the head of the church, his body, of which he is the Savior." What God has for me and my family I desire! As time passed I decided we should have a big wedding and Craig agreed because that's what I always wanted, but I wanted the love as well! I wanted to do right by our marriage. It just felt like a fresh start. During the first wedding he was locked up, for the second wedding we were at church, but no one really showed up. So I wanted the next wedding to be special. I would finally have the wedding of my dreams. God's grace is sufficient. The Bible says in Psalm 37:3-4 (NLT), "Trust in the Lord and do good then you will live safely in the land and prosper. Take delight in the Lord and He will give you your heart's desires."

CHAPTER 8
In Too Deep

I feel I need to talk about this one topic because a lot of people are dealing with situations of abuse from men and from women. One day my husband and I went joyriding; the kids were in the house with my sister. I let Craig drive my car. He used to get mad if I didn't let him drive. We stopped at a red light and he was staring this girl up and down like she was a smothered pork chop. Mind you, he already made me feel insecure about myself. He made me feel that I was not really what he wanted, but he'd stay with me until he found what he was looking for.

Sometimes people don't tell you their true intentions. To be disrespected while I was with him showed me he didn't really care for me like he said he did. His words and his actions weren't lining up. I was boiling inside. I got teary-eyed and I don't like showing my emotions, letting anyone know they hurt me, so I popped him on the right side of his face.

He balled up his fist and hit me hard in my mouth, then my tooth came out! I just sat there in disbelief like, *Did he really ball up his fist and hit me?* I was trying to figure out what to do. In my head I was rambling. *Do I call the police, go to the hospital or call my mother?* He tried to justify what he'd done. I hit him first, yes, but it wasn't a ball up your fist blow, it was more like an "aut, aut, baby don't do that. Don't play with her." Neither of them were right, but there is a difference! I told him to take me to the Hospital, so he drove me to PG Hospital. He said, "Now I'm about to go to jail."

When we got to the Hospital, he jumped out of the car, got on his knees in the middle of the street and prayed. I felt like God was telling me to forgive him, so I went into the hospital. They wanted to know off bucks was it domestic violence, and I really wanted to say yeah, but can you imagine lying to the doctor and the person that did it is right there hearing you lie for them? I told the doctors that someone was trying to fix my car, pulled on the door handle and elbowed me in my mouth. I could not believe what I'd just said. The guilt he made me feel by saying I shouldn't have hit him made me feel like I deserved it! I felt like God must really be dealing with me through this.

The doctor prescribed pain medication and told me to see my dentist in the morning to save my tooth. I had to go home and he was still driving my damn car. I said to myself, *How stupid can I be?* He kept trying to talk to me, but I really had had enough of his sh*t for the night.

I got in my house and my sister Brina knew something was wrong, but did not come to see if I was okay. I gave my kids a hug. Tears came down my face as I was walking away. They are flowing right now as I'm typing. I went to my room and took a look in the mirror and realized I had just been robbed of my beautiful smile. I had straight pearly whites.

I believe he was jealous of me. I always felt like he tried to break my spirit down and make me feel less than, so no one else would want me and he was okay with that. The burn on my head played a major part in my life in what I allowed to happen; he knew I didn't like showing people my burn. That's how I fell for him. He's the one that knew about my burn and still wanted to be around, but little did I know he had his own intentions as to why he was with me. I just couldn't see it yet!

I went to the dentist the next morning. They took me as an emergency and they got right to the questions. "Were you hurt due to domestic violence?" Then I said, "No ma'am." She replied, "Then what happened?" Finally I said, "Someone was fixing my car and I was bent down and as they pulled the door open they elbowed me in my mouth."

I couldn't believe I was memorizing a lie. All I wanted was for them to say that they could fix my tooth. She walked out the room for a while. When she came back she had good news: They could put the tooth back in my mouth, but I would have to wear a splint on it for about six months. It looked like I had some jacked up braces but it was only on one side of my mouth. I can honestly tell you I didn't smile for a long time.

My spirit was very low and I didn't feel like myself anymore. I didn't want to talk to anybody. Most of my personality is in my smile, and I'd been robbed of it. People used to ask what happened to my teeth and I told them part of the truth, that it was just braces. I felt like when I talked to Craig after that happened things were different. I didn't wanna make him mad. I realized he had a temper problem. Maybe I had one as well. Not making any excuses as to why this happened to me, but all of it was wrong. I felt like I was in bondage, not free to be myself. I can't even tell you the last time I felt like myself, probably before I met Craig. I believe I lost myself a long time ago when I was last seen at the age of fifteen.

Sometimes I think I stayed with him so long because of my family. I wanted to do right by God and fight for my family, but the enemy was making me think I couldn't get out. I felt like if I left, no one else was gonna want me. I thought to myself, *I'm not strong enough to leave. He will change eventually. I need him, he is my protection.* As y'all know I got raped, so I felt every man

79

was out to get me. I did not trust anyone and the one I did trust had just turned on me. *What am I supposed to do now?*

I honestly believe you should try to be nice to everyone you meet because you never know what they are going through. Try to be the solution and not another problem. My mistake was putting trust in man instead of God. Scripture says in Psalm 146:3-9 (NLT), "Don't put your confidence in powerful people; there is no help for you there. When they breathe their last, they return to the earth, and all their plans die with them. But joyful are those who have the God of Israel as their helper, whose hope is in the Lord their God. He made heaven and earth, the sea, and everything in them. He keeps every promise forever. He gives justice to the oppressed and food to the hungry. The Lord frees the prisoners. The Lord opens the eyes of the blind. The Lord lifts up those who are weighed down. The Lord loves the godly. The Lord protects the foreigners among us. He cares for the orphans and widows, but he frustrates the plans of the wicked."

Give God your weakness and He'll give you His strength. In Jeremiah 30:17 (New International

Version) it says, "I will restore you to health and heal your wounds, declares the Lord."

CHAPTER 9
Leading By Example

I was in a place in my life where tough decisions and sacrifices had to be made. I had to apply for TANF (Temporary Assistance for Needy Families) because I needed food stamps and cash assistance to provide for my family. TANF instructed me that in order for me to receive the benefits, I would have to go through a program and that they were no longer assisting people who were sitting on their behinds. I could understand that; in fact, it was just the push I needed.

In order to receive the benefits from the government, I had to choose between one option or another. The government told me I either had to get my diploma or go to a workshop every day until I got a job. I knew I didn't want to go to the workshop for five hours every day, so I did what I thought was best. I didn't even want to go back to school to be honest. After comparing the two, eventually, I decided to sign up for school. The government official told me it could take a month or so to get enrolled in school. On the other hand God had something else in store.

The next day I received a phone call saying there was a spot available for me to get enrolled. I was dazed, after that phone call I was mad as heck! I was shocked by the news so I felt mixed emotions: I was shocked and nervous. I wasn't the only one starting school, my children and I were starting on the same day. I realized I had to be the example for my children. My children knew I didn't graduate high school, so I knew that this was my chance to be the example. To show that if I could do it, then they could do it too.

Going back for me was a challenge because there were so many barriers in my way trying to stop me from going, so I made excuses. Making excuses was like second nature to me. Especially when I wasn't that excited about facing the challenges ahead. But the pressure was on me because my kids were watching me, not to mention I had two jobs as well.

My job was very demanding because I worked with people that had special needs. I always had a busy schedule, from me waking up in the morning and making breakfast for my children, to me driving them to school. After that I had to get to my first class at 9 in the morning and it lasted until 2 in the afternoon for my last class. In between lunch breaks I completed my homework from all my other classes.

When school was over I had to get to my first job, which was working with Ant. I got a second job because my aunt realized I was working with Ant. My aunt Missy didn't want anyone to work for her except me. For my first job I was working from 4 to 10 p.m. I was working with my aunt on the weekends from 9 a.m. to 5 p.m. My aunt Missy had a disability as well. I was going back and forth between jobs because my aunt Missy didn't really want me working with Ant. So I had to switch my schedule up.

While I was attending school I took the train and I left my car home because it was getting unbearable to pay for parking every day. I got a phone call during class one day from the police. Now before I tell you about what the officer said, I'm gonna give you some history.

Craig crashed my truck before, so I used my tax money to get it repaired and refurbished. My truck got new tints, new rims and a new paint job; it looked like a brand new truck. I allowed him to drive and I suffered because of that. I was injured from the previous car accident. I was in a rental car with Craig's cousins Lisha and Ant, which by the way I was on the clock for my job. We were headed to North Carolina to visit my sister Brina, but we did not make it.

A fourteen wheeler truck side swiped me and took the entire door off my rental car. We ended up going to the Hospital and we were all in pain. My neck was killing me and the next day my body started to swell. I was in so much pain, not to mention we could have died. Craig's cousin who has been my friend for fifteen years decided the money was better than our relationship. She had a lawsuit against me for one million dollars. Can you believe that? Money makes people do foolish things, especially losing a real one. I knew changes were ahead. I had to go through therapy for several weeks and all.

Now that I got you up to speed here is what the officer said while I was in school. The officer asked, "Is this Keonna Young?" I replied, "Yes." Then the officer asked, "Is Craig your husband?" I replied, "Yes, is he okay?" The officer responded, "Ma'am, we have Mr. Young here in the Washington Hospital Center. He's been involved in a five-car pile up accident. He was driving your GMC Yukon XL. He was high on PCP and crashed into three parked cars and one car with two passengers in the vehicle."

I'm surprised he didn't go to jail. My car got totaled, I got served a lawsuit against me and my insurance company because Craig drove my car without permission. When the dust settled, Craig didn't offer me any money or anything. I was back to square one, but Ant's mother, Cyn, stepped in and helped me by cosigning for a car. Cyn told me if she did a cosign that I better not let Craig drive the car. I had at least $1500 in my bank account, but Cyn used her credit because I didn't have any credit.

While that was happening I still managed to spend time with my Children. Of course I was dealing with a lot of obstacles. There were thoughts running through my head telling me I couldn't do it, I was not good enough or smart enough, thinking that I don't have what it takes. But my struggles or thoughts didn't stop me. However, the more steadfast I became, the more I found out about myself. I didn't like being late to anything or not being prepared when it came to school. So I made sure I would prepare the night before.

I discovered I love writing, and I also love being around people who are just like me. I realized going back to school wasn't that bad after all. Even my classmates encouraged me and others to keep going when times got tough. We all need that extra push to get us over that hump that tried to stop us from finishing our goal. It is never too late to follow your dreams. God pushed me, from visualizing the goal to making it happen. I felt proud when I would do my homework and be on time for school. It was like I was stepping up to the plate and meeting my destiny.

In the end I graduated not only with a 3.6 GPA, but because of my GPA, I also was awarded the honor of being the Salutatorian. I got to give a speech to everyone at the graduation ceremony. I had stage fright, but I delivered my speech in excellent fashion. Even my speech was new to me because I'd never done it before. It felt good to look into the audience and see my children watching me graduate. In my heart I felt like in spite of all the trials I had to go through to get to that very moment, it was worth it. Only thing I could say about it looking back was God made it happen.

Completing High School was one of my greatest accomplishments. Without the people God placed in my life I wouldn't have excelled as much as I did. Moral of this story is: If God brought you to it, He will bring you through it! Scripture says in Isaiah 41:10 (NIV), "So do not fear, for I am with you; do not be dismayed, for I am your God. I will strengthen you and help you; I will uphold you with my righteous right hand."

CHAPTER 10
The SnowBall Effect 2020

My family and I, including Isaiah, were living in SouthEast at the time in the middle of Mellon St and MLK. This day there was a lot going on. Craig was high again and was scaring my children with a loud outburst. He said, "Ain't nobody leaving this house or I'm gonna blow this b*tch up." I replied, "Oh no you not!" I had to try to get him out the house without getting him more amped so we wouldn't end up fighting. God was on my side.

Craig decided to stand on the porch and glare at the neighbors, who were being all nosey. That was my open door to lock him out. "Thank you, Lord!" Angel said to me, "Mom, please don't let him back in. I hate when he's high, he scares me for real." Craig decided to bang on the door and said, "Let me in *now!*" causing a scene. I didn't let him in. I told him to come back when he was sober and then I'd let him in. No, I wasn't kicking him out; he just had to realize we weren't safe when he was on them drugs. Trust me, I know!

Another time he was high and I had to kick him out. I felt bad for him and decided to get him some water. I grabbed a water bottle and opened the screen door to hand him the water. Then he pressed his foot on the door while I was giving it to him. He knew exactly what he was doing. I could see the evil in his eyes while he was trying to snap my arm. That's a whole nother story that's too long.

Craig went somewhere after he realized I wasn't letting him in. I didn't hear from or see him for like five hours. I finally received a phone call and it was not Craig, it was a police officer calling about Craig. I couldn't catch a break. The officer said they had my husband at Prince

George's hospital. He'd gotten robbed at the corner of our home and pistol whipped. Then the officer handed the phone to Craig. I asked Craig if he was okay and did he know who did this to him. Craig said he didn't know, he couldn't remember anything. The police said they didn't know when he would be released, and on top of that whoever did it took his phone. The officer said it looked to be a hate crime and they asked if we would need to be in protective custody. I told the officers, "Yes!"

I had been having trouble around that neighborhood for awhile. Someone put a gun to my oldest son's and Isaiah's head and robbed them. The boys that robbed them said they had been watching us. I couldn't believe it. I worked hard for my money and for my family to make sure they have what they need and there were people plotting to take it from us. Yes, please move me. God was giving us an exit.

Due to COVID Craig could not have visitors. I got on the phone and told his family and my mother what was going on. When Greg got home his brothers came and stayed with us. Craig had a big knot on his forehead and on the back of his head, not to mention the stitches. The police reserved a hotel for my family. We had to gather some of our belongings and go. We couldn't tell anyone where we were headed.

They gave us a forty-five day stay until we could find somewhere else to live. Everything was happening so fast. While all of that was going on, I paid for plane tickets because I had to get a BBL surgery done. I needed to get my surgery done a few days after we moved to the hotel. The main point of my BBL was for my hips. I had none. I wanted a little something to make me feel beautiful. As crazy as it seems my husband's eyes were never on me, they were on everyone else that was thicker than me. He really made me feel ugly or not good enough. So I decided when I did get my surgery done it wouldn't be for him. I was gonna let him keep looking at other chicks.

Craig wasn't at his best after what he'd been through; he was paranoid. I couldn't blame him. I kept asking him if he remembered anything that happened to him, but he said couldn't. Craig was very angry and I was too. We also got a storage unit before I caught my flight. I needed all of my money, but guess who had to pay for everything including my *ss. Yep! *This girl.* So yeah like I said, he can keep looking at them other chicks.

My children stayed in the hotel and they were happy about that. After everything was settled with the storage unit and the emergency move, Craig and I were headed to Miami, Florida to get my surgery done. When we arrived they checked my weight and made sure my money was all paid up. They asked me to take my clothes off so they could see what needed to be done. The doctor asked if I wanted a Nikki Manaj butt. I said, "No, ma'am. I mainly want hips; as you can see they are nowhere to be found." She told me don't eat or drink past 8 p.m.

So pretty much after I got into the hotel, my first night was cut early in Miami. Craig and I woke up and took a walk around a little to get our minds right from what was going on at home. It is so beautiful in Florida. At 7 a.m. the next day I was up preparing for my phat butt. We caught a cab and went to get my surgery done. They took me in the back and told Craig he could not stay in the waiting room because of COVID, so he left.

I went in the back and they had me lay on this table. They strapped my hands and feet to the table and gave me a needle. The doctor said I was gonna be out very soon and that everything was gonna be okay. But before my eyes closed I saw another doctor come in to do the surgery or help out. That didn't sit well with me because the doctor I chose to do my surgery was based on the reviews people left. I did not see the reviews on the other doctor, but I was already drowsy and just like that I was out.

When I woke up I was in so much pain. I didn't even have time to wake up fully. I couldn't speak just yet. I was bleeding profusely and I was getting tossed into a cab on my stomach and my husband had to get me out by himself. I was in tears. The doctors said it was gonna be painful but the medicine should help alleviate the pain. That was a lie! I didn't have feeling in my hands.

I asked Craig to call the doctor and see if that was normal. The doctor said it was normal, so I just got some rest and prepared for the next day of the re-evaluation. The next day I was getting phone calls from my children and text messages with videos showing that my house was getting robbed and on top of that, it was my oldest son Damonte's friend that I fed and allowed in my home. He went on family trips with us and I treated him like one of my own. I could not believe this sh*t. Not right now, I couldn't even do anything. I felt helpless.

My mom called the police and reported it, but to watch people on video run out of your home with your belongings really hurts. I could not believe that little mother freaker was biting the hand that fed him. *Lord, what is going on? I can't even heal in peace.*

After all of that chaos was going on it finally was packing day. The doctor cleared me to go and I was ready. I was still in so much pain. I was trying to figure out how I was gonna sit on the plane if the doctor didn't want me to sit on my butt. We went in a cab to go to the airport. My funds were getting really low and I had no help with that from Craig.

We got to the airport an hour before the flight and checked in, mind you, I had to stand the whole time and the devil was not letting up. They said the flight was packed and they didn't have another flight until 6 p.m. I thought, *That's freaking nuts! What am I supposed to do until then?* I was weak, I'd just had surgery, and I could not sit on my butt. I had the butt pillow but I was not allowed to sit on my butt for long. Who pays all that money to get a dent in it? I think not.

So I decided to pay for another hotel room at the airport which, by the way, came up to $87.00 for 4 hours. I only had $30 left to my name, so they needed to get me on that plane. I was very hungry and I had to eat something. I had some medicine in my system.

I can't lie, Craig was taking really good care of me after my surgery. Craig made sure he kept my mother in the loop every step of the way and I appreciated that. He also made sure I got my medicine, even in the middle of the night. It was the most I'd seen Craig want to be supportive without making an excuse to leave. When it was time for us to leave the hotel so we could get on the flight back to DC, another delay happened. The devil is a liar! They pushed the flight back to 10 p.m. I was pissed and on top of that I had no more money. I had to call my mom and my sister Bella.

My mom Cash App'd me some money and she even called up her friends so I could get a rental car to get to her. My sister Bella even chipped in. Thank you, Jesus. I'm so over Miami's airport. It's the worst, in my opinion. We got a van and Craig put the seats down flat to the floor so I could lay flat on my stomach. Now instead of going straight home, we stopped at my mom's house. We stayed for an hour and a half. She fed us and guess what, she let us keep her Yukon truck to ride to DC. That was a blessing because it meant we wouldn't have to stress over the rental and where to drop it off.

My mom came through. This was special for me because my history with my mom was always pay for this and pay for that. Not this time. It felt like I just had my mommy. Thank you, God. After 11 hours on the road we were finally back to the hotel. We got news that the police blocked the back door with my couch.

The children were happy to see me. They could not wait to see what I wanted them to do. I'm gonna be honest, at first I wanted him beat up. But what was that gonna solve? It wouldn't change the fact that he broke into my house. I also thought these little ones were looking for mom to make the right decision. So, I chose life and let the police handle it. I didn't want the enemy to use my decision to his advantage. Every time I made the right choice, the devil lost power over me. I just gave y'all a jewel right there, hold on to it.

The children went back to their room while Craig and I had our own room. I went and lay down for over 20 hours. The police called my phone and let us know they would patrol the block until we came back to town. I did not want them to know I was back just yet, I was too tired.

I noticed while laying down I couldn't lay on my stomach for more than 7 minutes. My arms felt like I had pins and needles in them. It was unbearable. I had to stand up in the middle of the night in the middle of the hotel floor because the pain was excruciating. I could not sleep! I was standing up crying. So many questions came to my head: *Did they do something wrong during the surgery? Was God punishing me for something?*

When I started thinking some more, I wondered, *Did I even ask God for his permission?* The Bible says, "Acknowledge God in all thy ways and He shall direct thy path" (Proverbs 3:6). I started beating myself up, asking God for forgiveness. I'm telling you it felt like I was getting the wrath of God. I felt heat coming from my entire body. My hands felt like needles that tingle, like when you stay on the toilet for a long time and your foot goes to sleep. Yeah, I felt that non-stop.

Craig was trying to help, but he was sleepy too. So it was just me and God. I called my mom crying. She told me to call that doctor in the morning to find out what was going on with me. They said they would need to see me. I knew I was not going back to Florida, so I ended up going to the hospital. The doctor at the hospital said I had nerve damage in both of my hands, one more than the other. The doctor gave me some strong medicine. He said it should help. I didn't even mention that when I tried to lift my hands up over my head, the pain went straight to a 10.

I was so scared to hear the doctor say I would need to do physical therapy, not to mention I was out of money because of all the things that were going on. I had to get lymphatic massages on my stomach. I got the money from my dad to get my massage because if I didn't, I would have fibrosis in my stomach. It cost $115.00 dollars. The decisions I made came with a price. I couldn't put my arms where the therapist needed them to be, and she noticed I was still swollen. She told me she couldn't do the massages on me due to the swelling; something else was going on.

Let's just say the hospital visits became consistent. The medicine the doctor prescribed was not working. Craig said, "Stink, I'm not trying to be funny, but I think you need some weed. Weed relaxes muscles and blocks pain." I haven't smoked marijauna in over 8 years. On the other hand, I was willing to try anything at that moment. So we put everything that we were dealing with on the back burner and called my bro from another mother and he gave me some weed.

I smoked it as soon as I got it to see if it would really help. Omg, it blocked the pain. I still felt the tingle in my hands but no pain. I could finally get some sleep. I knew it was too good to be true. The pain came back once my high wore off. *That's not good, that means the enemy is putting me back in bondage.* Think about it, I would have to keep smoking the weed that I was free from for 8 years to become addicted again. Something had to give.

Craig was more excited about me smoking again because we were doing drugs together. It's crazy that my own husband didn't want better for us. We were becoming more and more unequally yoked. I wanted better for my family and myself. A lot of thoughts started to run through my mind. Craig realized I wasn't smoking just for the fun of it. I was only smoking when the pain came. Craig started leaving me, and I had to fend for myself. Now that's the Craig I know. When I needed him the most he flaked out on me. I took it as "what didn't kill me made me stronger." I'd had enough of Craig's BS.

We had to go check out our house in SouthEast. The damage the robbers did was crazy! When some of the robbers that were on the video were my neighbors and my son's friend, that hit differently. When we arrived their eyes were glued to us. I think they were looking for a reaction, but you reap what you sow. When we opened the door I saw that my fish were dead. They had put detergent in the tank among other things. They set toilet paper on fire upstairs.

They used my house to smoke and have sex in. They left used condoms on the floor in Angel's room. They put a hole in the wall, they took my spiritual scriptures and ripped them up. They wrote on the walls and they even took the majority of my appliances and clothes. At that point I did not feel like picking through trash because that's what it was after all the damage. We grabbed the microwave and tookit to the hotel. The hotel didn't have a microwave so we gained something in a way.

We got news that my granddaughter was born on October 17, 2021. My oldest son was a father and his baby's mom did not want to go home because she was a foster child. I couldn't even imagine what her story was. So Miracle ended up coming with us. We barely had room for us, but I was excited to be a grandma and she was the light in this storm. Every time I spent time with her she brought me joy, nothing else mattered.

My time was coming to an end at the hotel, but we couldn't find a place within 45 days. They ended up giving us an extension of 15 days. We still couldn't find a house. Finally, when our extension was up we had to leave for good.

The good thing was we still had my mom's truck plus my van. We packed up and I made some phone calls to make sure my children had a place to stay. Sean and Adrian stayed with their uncle, Craig's brother. Angel went over to her best friend Kay's house and switched to her boyfriend's house when she wanted to give her best friend's family a breather. My oldest son Damonte and Isaiah went over to their friend's house for a while, but that ran out quickly. I ended up asking Craig's cousin Lisha if they could stay at her house until we found a house. I really appreciated that. Miracle had to go back to where she came from, but she wanted the baby to stay with me. Craig and I were the only ones with nowhere to go. Craig, my granddaughter and I had to sleep in the van. We laid the chairs back as far as they would go into the floor, put blankets down with pillows and made it work. When we had to use the bathroom we went to a restaurant or stopped at Lisha's to shower.

In the midst of our snowball effect, God always had His hands on us and covered us. If He did it for me in spite of all my decisions, He will do it for you too. So do not fear, for I am with you; do not be dismayed, for I am your God. I will strengthen you and help you; I will uphold you with my righteous right hand (Isaiah 41:10). "Cast all your anxiety on Him because He cares for you" (1 Peter 5:7).

CHAPTER 11
God Blocked It, Again

Where to begin... Minding my business in a CVS parking lot turned into a nightmare. After being homeless and living in my van for about two weeks, I was in a CVS parking lot with my husband, my daughter and my newborn granddaughter. My daughter was only visiting me because she missed us. We decided to stop driving around and wasting gas. I really wanted to get some rest, but I couldn't do it because I had to look out for people walking past my car and interfering in my business. I was worried that they could call the police or social services and take my grandchild because we had nowhere to go.

A red truck pulled up right next to us, and I was wondering why would the driver want to squeeze right beside us when there was much more space in the parking lot. In the red truck there was a guy on the passenger side and a woman on the driver side. We looked at the car for a moment, but went back to what we were doing.

I was on the phone with my mom, mind you. The guy jumped out from the passenger side of the car and he said something, but I barely heard what he said because our windows were rolled up. Craig was on the driver side and the guy came up to Craig's window yelling, "Yeah n*gga! What the f**k are you looking at?" I looked at Craig and said, "What the f**k; is he high? Do you hear him?" Craig, with a confused look on his face, replied, "He was talking to me?" Then he told me to chill. Craig said, "He must have a gun." The guy who was yelling at Craig's window overheard Craig and said, "I don't have no gun, n*gga!" Craig said, "You don't have a gun? Oh yeah!" Craig opened the door and while the door was opening Craig's fist was going across the man's face at the same time. Craig grabbed his throat and pushed him to the ground.

At that moment I was like, *Wow*. Mind you, I was on Facetime with my mom, so I flipped the camera around so she could see too. Man, Craig beat the mess out of him on some slight s**t ! I bet you he wishes he'd never done that big goofy s**t. He learned that day! That's crazy that I got turned on by that. I love a man that can hold his own.

However, looking back I realized that I was turned on by the wrong things, especially violence. Don't get me wrong a protector is good, but the word says you shouldn't render evil for evil. We could've easily moved when they came beside us. Thinking like that shows maturity, especially when you grow in the word.

After the fight the girl in the driver seat got out of the car and told her dude, "Come on, let's just go!" Craig picked up the dude's glasses and gave them back to him. I said, "I don't know why you came at us like that anyway. Like you tough; you don't know what people are going through. That's why you should have minded your business, got your a** whooped. Then the girl said to me, "I'm a female, bi**h, I will whoop your a**." I said to her, "I doubt that!" She pulled out a gun and pointed it at me in broad daylight.

In my head I thought about what my daughter must have been thinking when a gun got pointed towards me while Craig was trying to defuse the situation. I told that girl I don't fear anybody but God! All of the things I already faced in my life. I didn't want to leave my children behind, but please don't threaten me with meeting my maker! Her dude told her to get back in the car.

Craig and I got back in my van and drove off, but it wasn't over yet. They started following us so Craig had to do some maneuvering, but we got out of there by the grace of God. There was another gun in my face, the devil wanted me dead but God said no. God blocked it! Scripture says in Isaiah 54:17, "No weapon that is formed against thee shall prosper; and every tongue that shall rise against thee in judgment thou shalt condemn."

CHAPTER 12
Enough Is Enough

I was completely lost in what was going on with my
family and I. Ms. Mya (my case manager) called my
phone and asked if I was ready to go to the family
shelter. She said she needed 24-hour notice for intake.
I told Ms. Mya to give me a second to think about it.
The reason I had to think about it was because I already
had a voucher to get another house, so I was in disbelief
as to why I had to go to the shelter. I was in the car
listening to Erica-isms on the radio, and she delivered
a great message saying to stay focused on my craft and
ask God, Why am I here? Whatever God has me in
right now I need to stay focused and always remember
what is my "why."

A light bulb clicked in my head and the Holy Spirit was saying, *Turn to your left.* When I looked to my left I saw the shelter. I was looking at all of the windows and the Spirit kept speaking to me. Look at the bigger picture: How many souls can be saved in this building alone? At that very moment I realized it was bigger than us...way bigger! God is a good God! He didn't just rescue my family. God said, "You are on assignment not a rescue mission!" Amen to that!

The Lord had to remind me that I am the salt in the earth and wherever He wants to take me, I am and have to be His willing vessel. I love the Lord and trust that my steps are ordered on good ground. I told Ms. Mya, my family and I were ready to go into the shelter. It had my mind wondering what to expect. Television can give you the wrong impression of things. How would it be when we got there? Is it dirty? Is it safe? How's the food? Is there privacy? What's the curfew? You have to keep this stuff in mind going into an environment you haven't been to in a while. I was in a shelter in the early 2000's when I had only my son Damonte and my daughter Angel; they were only toddlers at the time.

I looked around and saw that my grandchild Kayla and my husband were sleeping in the van. There were times when Kayla was with me in the car and times she was with Angel over at her boyfriend's house. Although it wasn't Angel's responsibility (Kayla wasn't her child), she was still willing to step up to the plate. My children were separated from me because we were homeless, so that's a definite yes for me to go through the unknown! After 2 months of staying in a hotel, the government stopped paying for our stipend. With no house found yet to fit my family's requirements, we all had to go our separate ways for a while. Damonte and Isaiah were in an abandoned school building and ended up staying with Craig's cousin and my daughter Angel was staying over her boyfriend's house and my son Sean and Adrian stayed with his uncle on Craig's side of the family. Something gots to give. I just knew God had an exit. (Enough is enough, I'll take anything right now just to have my family back with me. We never separate, if anything other children gravitate to our family.

The next day we went to the family shelter and my children were really happy to be with each other again; we weren't used to being separated. The only one that had a problem was my oldest son Damonte. He had an attitude and when I asked him what was wrong, he said, "Living in a shelter isn't for me." Which is crazy talk. What, does he think he's better than everyone else? The rest of us had to stay in the shelter. So what was he implying?

I couldn't understand why he thought like that because when we helped the homeless, did he think they were below us? I believe my son was avoiding the revelation God was trying to show us through our trials. Even though Damonte felt that way, as a mom I knew I had to protect him by adding him to my case so he would have a place to stay when the streets stopped loving him. I wanted to tell him, but I knew he had to go through it. The streets don't love nobody.

When we checked into the shelter they took our clothes to steam them from bed bugs or anything else to protect us. That right there showed me the shelter was safe from bed bugs. When we got inside our room I saw we had a double room connected. There were windows with a good view, so I could look at my van across the street. From that right there God was showing me that He really knows what He is doing.

There were five beds in one room with a dresser for each bed and a mini fridge. The room I was staying in had three beds, a playpen for my grandchild, a bathroom and a wardrobe. All in all, it was the complete opposite of what we thought it would be like. The staff welcomed us, the building was clean, the floor we were on was quiet and from time to time we would see people go into their rooms.

They even knew we needed clothes, so they got right on it. They took Angel and me to a place where you can get clothes for your family. You check the sizes and the brands. It's hard to believe, but the clothes were new. I can honestly say we only had trouble with one of our case managers in the shelter. She barely helped us or wasn't in the building.

So thank God, He was on our side! God does stuff in His timing, also when you think God is not with you He really is. God literally ministers to you in your dark places! While I'm going through the storm, He's leading the way. Thank you, Jesus! God is an amazing God!

CHAPTER 13
His Omnipresence

It was December 20, 2020 on a Sunday morning. We weren't supposed to go to church because of the pandemic. As you know the government closed down the churches, which I couldn't understand. In the Bible it says obey the laws of the land, but this particular Sunday the Spirit told me to go. I'd rather obey God than the government. When I used to follow people they would steer me the wrong way, but I've learned to trust God and allow Him to guide me.

When the Spirit told us to go to church, once we arrived, we saw that service had already begun. So I decided to plug my phone up to my speaker in the van so we wouldn't miss anything the Spirit wanted us to listen to. There was a lady singing for praise and worship, but the phone kept losing signal. The devil is a liar! I did not let that stop me, knowing that it was the devil trying to shut my mouth so I wouldn't be able to praise my God! I think not! I have to go in!

I know that when I praise God my troubles will soon fade away. I might have cried during my storms, but when I did cry, I cried out to the Lord and prayers were said. I didn't allow my problems to have me. The angels have been showing me and sending me messages through numbers on car tags. My family and I have witnessed these signs. I keep seeing eights everywhere. All of the numbers have different meanings, especially at different points in my life, which taught me to humble myself and enjoy the journey God is taking my family and me on. The eights represent abundance and it comes in different forms.

What I heard from the sermon is God was telling me I'm in a season of receiving help from others and that

God had me in a position to not only help my family, but also to pay attention to those around me that He placed in my space and in my path. That message reminded me of my spiritual animal, which is a turtle. The turtle symbolizes that slow and steady wins the race. Turtles can be slow, but they also teach us to walk our path in patience, peace, determination and serenity. It represents the ability to stay grounded, slow down, pace yourself and be persistent.

After the service was over a church member gave me an envelope. I didn't look inside of it, but I just knew it was a blessing because I remember seeing 8's that represent abundance. Then after I got blessed my kids were next, my son Sean and my daughter Angel got $50 each. When abundance takes place in your life it's not just for you, but it's for whoever you are connected to. I went to talk to the pastor after church, and I told him everything that was taking place with my family and I.

After the pastor heard what was going on, he asked me why I didn't tell him sooner. I replied, "Because I know I have the same power as you. I remember you taught me in the word that we all have the measure of faith, so I believe my prayers will do!" Pastor looked at me proudly and said, "Amen." I guess he realized that growth had taken its place in my life and the messages he preached were being received. I've realized trouble doesn't always last and when you stand on God's word and stay in prayer, God will make a way for you. Your job is to believe. Scripture says in Romans 10:17, "Faith comes by hearing and hearing by the word of God."

CHAPTER 14
No Compromise

Getting the shot, I think not! I went to work again last night and my supervisor was about to leave. She told me that she would send me the link so I could get my COVID shot. I told her I didn't want to get the COVID shot, but she said it was mandatory. Everyone has to get the shot if they are in healthcare. I still told her I'm not getting that shot, that's not gonna happen!

If someone compromises themselves or their beliefs, the enemy can toss them to and fro because they don't know what they want, which leads to confusion, and confusion is from the enemy. God told me never to compromise or settle for less, so I picked a side and stuck with it.

So I got in a car with Sean and Isaiah, and I told them what was going on at my job about the COVID shot and I started to cry real hard. I told Isaiah, "I didn't even cry this hard for Craig when we separated."

Craig had made it not so peaceful in my house from his drug use and the effects of that. Most of the time I didn't want to come home, so I just used to get in my car and drive away from the house or at least two blocks over just to find some peace. Sometimes I couldn't believe I was the one having to leave my house and not him. I felt like I was being smothered. I was overwhelmed, I felt like I didn't have anybody; I had pushed most people away. I isolated myself to try to keep my marriage and family together.

I guess I shouldn't have done that because when I wanted an outlet the enemy would talk to me and say, "You can't go to your family's house! It's gonna be like you only come around when you and Craig are going through something." I allowed the enemy to plant that seed in my spirit, and that was why I felt trapped!

Ladies, no matter what you are going through that others don't see, please don't allow the enemy to make you feel like you have nowhere to turn; most definitely call on the name of the Lord.

Craig still wanted to be around his friends and that was a no no because God already told him multiple times to stop hanging with them. He helped out with cooking, but that's because he liked to eat.

I would come home to nitpicking which led to arguing. He wasn't even doing his part around the house like simply cleaning up I feel as though that's the least he could've done as far as keeping the house clean. He could've made sure the kids were straight, and last but not least he shouldn't have picked fights with me when I got off of work. Especially since he wasn't helping me pay bills.

He always wanted to make excuses as to why he couldn't or wouldn't get a job. That's why I loved going to work, that's where I had peace. Yes, it is sad that I was doing almost everything. I started thinking, why was Craig laying in my bed if he wasn't carrying and pulling his weight or doing anything. The worst part of it was he wasn't really leading me to Christ. Was he really praying for me on a daily basis? Was he really encouraging me to study the Bible? No! I'm not judging, but it was like he was more attached to the worldly things than to God. That was making me feel like we were unequally yoked.

It was my job to pray and keep the faith though. I could say "I" all day, but what I failed at was I got tired of praying for someone who wasn't praying for me. Now as selfish as that sounds, it's my truth. I didn't even know how selfish that was until God told me. God asked me why I wasn't praying for something that I wanted changed? I felt like my test was, am I gonna keep letting the negative things happen and irritate my spirit or delay my destiny or my assignment to who God called me to be? There was too much weight on my shoulders.

It was time to let some of that baggage go! The thing is I didn't let it go on my own. I wanted to make sure that's what God wanted me to do. God allows us to make our own decisions by free will, but I rely more on what God says than what I think. So I would have to endure a whole lot of hardship in order for me to let it go easily when it was time. Or was I going to do something different?

I couldn't even get rest in the morning when I got off of work. He was laying in my damn bed while I was laying on a couch at work. Hmm, I paid $2700 for my bed and only got to sleep in it on the weekends. This crap ain't adding up at all! Then the Holy Spirit said my peace is with God! Amen! So Isaiah put on some of my favorite praise and worship songs as we were dropping Sean off to his girlfriend's house. The entire ride to his girlfriend's house we basked in God's presence through the gospel songs and the sun shining bright on us. After we dropped him off we got hungry so we went to IHOP but they weren't open. I wasn't really feeling like IHOP anyway, so I said, "Let's go to TGIF." I had a taste for some chicken Alfredo!

After we placed our order and got our food we went to the pawn shop which was in the same lot as TGIF. Before we even started talking about places where we could eat, I was debating whether I should pawn my wedding ring off. It was valuable in cash, but in my heart it had lost its value. Not to mention I needed the money for my car. My wedding ring was a white gold 2k double band. Craig had put up $300 to pay for mine, but that wasn't nearly enough for the full retail. So I went to go get that money, honey!

When I pawned the ring it made me feel like it was the next step to my destiny. After I pawned the ring Isaiah and I went back to the shelter to study because we were fasting and being obedient. How many of you know obedience is greater than sacrifice? Scripture says in 1 Samuel 15:22, "Listen! Obedience is better than sacrifice, and submission is better than offering the fat of rams."

CHAPTER 15
Unfinished Mission

It was a beautiful day to get outside of the shelter, so I decided to go outside and play. The Spirit led me to go to a friend of mine's house. My friend is a prophet. I usually have a good time visiting her and my Baltimore family, so I decided to text my friend Sherrice. I asked her if she was up for a visit. She said, "Yasssssss," with her hand lifted up in the air. Trust me I know her. She was always up for fellowship. She said, "Come on through, my sister, but I can't go outside. I've been in my word, God's not playing with me."

I already had intended to deliver a message to her that came from God. I realized He was trying to use me and I wanted to be obedient and help her because God had used my friend plenty of times when I needed to hear a word from Him. I was so thankful God allowed her to be there when I needed an encouraging spiritual sister. Some don't have those. I told Isaiah, God ain't tell me to stay away from her because God is love, and I am made in the image of God, so I am love as well.

I try my very best to do what's right. A great leader knows the way, goes the way and shows the way! Isaiah and I prayed before we left the shelter, and we prayed before we got inside the house knowing I have to deliver a message. We pulled up in front of her house. It was a narrow street that we could park on literally 3 steps away from her doorstep. It was a row house which means it was a house that was connected to other nearby houses.

As we were walking up to the door of her house my friend's oldest son stopped us and said before we came in we had to get anointed on our heads. That had my friend written all over it. I said, "Okay, but just so you know you don't have to touch people; you can just anoint the front door." As I walked in the door, I noticed a big hole in the wall in the living room. The hole is relevant because it shows that things were out of order.

I noticed that every time I visited my friend there was always something that God wanted me to see. One minute the lights were off, the next there was no food in the house or the stove wasn't working; there was always something. From the outside looking in, she had a house full of people and she was preaching the word to all of them. I couldn't see the fruit, so I could understand why the house was lacking. After I noticed all that God showed me, my spirit was on high alert. When I did come through she showed me a good time and always fed me. It's kind of contradictory, but when I came to visit she always told her Baltimore family to chip in to buy drinks, food and marijuana so we could have a good time.

Things had been changing for me, though, because I wasn't coming back as the same person or with the same intentions. Elevation was manifesting because I took more word in and died to my flesh. So when I was visiting I stopped smoking, but then each visit my flesh was dying gradually. I used to pray for her and myself because we all have problems, some more than others, so I felt empathetic. I knew I was on a mission though to tell her what God wanted me to say to her.

Back to the story. I went upstairs and my friend was on the floor praying, but she was twitching. I'd never seen her do that before, so I thought she was under a spirit that wasn't of God, like some kind of witchcraft. Scriptures were written all over her walls and the ceiling of her room with markers. There were two other people in the room with us, one guy and one girl; she'd had relationships with both of them in the past. God made sure there were two witnesses!

She got off the floor and she started saying stuff in reference to me, "Don't forget that you came to me for spiritual help." It wasn't actually my friend who provided the help, it was God using her, but everybody wants to take credit for things that God does. I wanted to say something, but I knew to let her keep speaking, usually that's the best way. If you allow people to speak long enough they usually tell you their true intentions.

She also started telling me I should be listening, but I thought I was. I even had enough respect to raise my hand while she was talking in order for me to ask a question or reply back. That shows growth because the old Keonna would have gone back and forth. My friend knew that, but she knew God had humbled me as well. She also told me that I'm not gonna win in life and this was coming from someone that had already prophesied over my life that I would be prosperous. So when things weren't going her way she came against mine. So who's the propheliar now?

You can't be loving one day , and the next day come against your sister in Christ. You can't be preaching the Word but still doing the opposite. Jesus said some people worship him with their lips instead of their heart. But be ye doers of the word, and not just hearers only, deceiving your own selves. (James 1:22) I knew right there off bucks a lot of things were off. That's why the Bible says test the spirit by the spirit. I knew this trip to her house had a purpose. I always get revelation after coming from her house. I've been around people who think just because they have been in the spiritual walk for a while or based on their age, they know more than you, but that's not true at all. The truth is if you are not humble enough to know that God can use anyone to get His message across then you're putting a limit on God. You have to be aware of God's omnipresence at all times.

You do not have to have a degree to get used by God, you just need to receive Jesus and you will be filled with the Holy Ghost. You also have to yield to the Spirit.

Do you know what I told her? I came against what she said and the devil that was talking to me through her: "I will win. God already told me I will!" I sensed a little hostility, jealousy and anger in her voice, especially since she was not speaking life. I got up and got ready to leave because she was doing too much. That was the second time I'd wasted my time going to her house and she wouldn't allow me to minister what God wanted me to say to his people because of her pride. Sherrice felt as though she knew more and I needed to fall back as she would say have several seats. We had our disagreement but I'm not about to keep wasting my gas and time so we ended up going to the store. Angel and Isaiah went to the store with me and Sherrice. We wanted to shop for clothes. When we went into the store it was this lady that was looking at us and I was trying to figure out why she was looking at us. The lady and her friend started to come towards us. She started prophesying to my friend and I continued walking. I knew we would be there longer if I had come, so I went and got the underclothes that I needed. When I was done I went where my friend Sherrice was and the lady must have been a prophet. She was definitely staring me down and she started speaking to me and said, "God told me to tell you to keep dancing". I almost dropped to my knees but instead I started to dance right there. They got to praying we paid for the things and left the store. I can't make this up. The lady that was prophesying asked my daughter and Isaiah what their relationship was to me. Angel replied, "I'm her daughter." The prophet asked if Angel would accept a hug from her just because she was related to me. Then Angel and the prophet friend hugged and talked to each other. The prophet turned to Isaiah and asked him how he is related to me. Isaiah responded, "I'm her son." Then the prophet said, "Don't be afraid to get close to your mother. Make sure you watch over her. Everybody can't touch her. If someone does try to touch her make sure you sanitize her hands." At that point I didn't know who I was. I knew I just wanted to do God's will.

I guess God told His prophet to say one more thing before she left. The prophet said unto me, "You not only the mother of Angel or Isaiah, you are the mother of all of them." As she said those words out of her mouth she spun around pointing at everyone who was remotely close to us. I guess when my friend heard that message from the prophet, it struck a nerve in her. She even hauled tail around the prophet as the Prophet was speaking.

People have to stop honoring the title more than the assignment God gave us. After the message a couple of days went by until Isaiah and I came back to Baltimore to visit again. This time when we came back we were on an assignment. I spoke to my friend and she told me that she was restricting her children from leaving the house. She was paranoid to go anywhere because she was tryna dodge the destruction because she ignored her warnings. Even with her paranoia she still had pride in her. She was still trying to speak in authority but wasn't leading nor being the example. She can have the "title" of authority, I just wanted her to stop hindering God's people from developing. I just wanted to do God's will. I felt like Moses telling her to let God's people go.

I told Sherrice I'm leaving and she jumped up and told me, "No, you're not. You're gonna stay right here with me!" Then she put her arm across the door to stop me from leaving her room. I told her, "If you don't get yo a** off of me, b**ch. I'm leaving this house!" I know I shouldn't have said that but I'd been getting my buttons pushed since I got there. Even at the door she should've put the oil on herself.

She was so used to getting her way with the people that lived with her, she must've forgotten who she was talking to. I stormed downstairs and out the door; I was so angry that she'd done that again. Seemed to me that she was fighting between herself and God and playing both sides of the fence. I'm not a judge, but from looking at her it seemed like she had gotten lost along the way. I won't give up on her, but she won't disrespect me. Eventually God will bring me back because He told me I am on a assignment and I'm a doer of the word!

Once I was in the car with Isaiah getting ready to leave, she came to the driver side of my car, knocking on the window, telling me to open the door. I told her, "No, I'm not opening the door." When she heard that she got in front of my car so I couldn't move. I told her, "Get out of the way or I will drive." While this was going on all of her family came outside to witness what was going on. She lived with 6 other people and all of them were at her doorstep shocked at what they were seeing.

She came back to the window and opened the car door from the back and tried to grab me, hug me and tell me she loved me. I don't think she really knows what love is. I know I didn't truly know what love was either, but I knew it wasn't what she was doing. I was already angry and I didn't want her to touch me, so I told her, "Get the f**k off me, b**ch."

When she finally got out of the way she tried to tell me she loved me again. I pulled off from her house with\ the tires making a *skurtt* sound. Her house was a minute away from the highway. I got on the highway driving like a maniac. I was engulfed in my flesh, there were spirits on me that needed to go away. Isaiah yelled at me, "Stop the car!"

I pulled over to the side of the road and I got out of the car. Isaiah told me not to allow her to make me angry. I screamed to the top of my lungs. Isaiah got out of the car and told me to dust my feet off, and then he hugged me. His hugs are the best and he does this thing where he puts his forehead on my forehead... it made me calm down. The energy he gives when he's near is out of this world.

We went home and did our daily studies and talked more about what happened, reflecting on how we could have handled things differently. It was an important assignment because I wasn't just going after my friend, I was going for God's children. We all need to understand that we are not supposed to hold God's children hostage but point them towards God and let Him order their steps. We're only supposed to pray for them and give them the word. Scripture says in Luke 18:16, "Then Jesus called for the children and said to the disciples, 'Let the children come to me. Don't stop them! For the Kingdom of God belongs to those who are like these children. I tell you the truth, anyone who doesn't receive the Kingdom of God like a child will never enter it.'"

CHAPTER 16
Temptation

A shift has taken place in the atmosphere! Am I losing myself? I'm confused. Wait... what did I just do? I cannot believe what just happened! It was night time and I shared a room with the boys at the shelter, so Isaiah and I pushed our beds together so we could have one big bed and be comfortable without falling off. The beds were small twin-size mats. May I add, the bed sheets wouldn't stay on. The reason I shared a room with the boys is because at the time Craig was still salty about the message from the Angel Number (999) that separated us. Not to mention he kept bothering and harassing me.

So I got up outta that room and rolled out! Isaiah and I did Bible study together and we looked at biblical movies because we were fasting and we were on the same page about accepting what God wanted from our lives. That's what really drew me to Isaiah; it was like a missing piece that finally was attached. I don't even know how or where to start.

Seeing the transition from me looking in the rear view mirror of my car heading to church on Sundays and seeing not even Craig or my children spiritually awoke, to the dramatic effect of how one conversion can make a difference. Let me say I felt so disgusted in the beginning because I had called this young man my son! Isaiah had been Damonte's best friend since 5th grade. God gave me Isaiah to guide him the right way. But in all actuality God is amazing because while I was helping him, he was helping me stay focused on my studies and pushing through for the dance ministry that God placed in my heart as well.

While we were in the shelter we practiced our dance routine. With that being said everyone knows or should understand that practice makes perfect. Practicing with a companion builds a relationship too. We even did a dance video when we got our routine correct in a week. He also helped me out every day, for example going with me to places like the grocery store. He helped me cook and helped me out with the other children. Isaiah was being a leader, leading like God called him to. There was temptation happening between Isaiah and me. We didn't even have these thoughts or feelings before about each other.

A week earlier Craig had mentioned that Isaiah liked me, but I never thought anything about it because I didn't think he did. I also spoke with Isaiah about that and he told me he never had feelings for me like that. Isaiah told me that I was his mom and I respected that because I thought of Isaiah as my son whom I loved very much and cared for like my very own. I knew Craig was trippin'! Craig opened his mouth and spoke about how he thought Isaiah and I were having sex. He pointed his fingers at us left to right, basically insinuating that we liked each other or that something was going on.

Life and death is in the power of your tongue and whatever you speak you might just manifest. Back to the moment we were in bed together, we got closer than ever before. He smelled really nice and he was rubbing my arm. He was rubbing my arm because he wanted to comfort me, especially after the events that had happened with Sherrice.

Also, that prophet asked me how Isaiah was related to me, and I told the prophet that he was my son. God was speaking to not only me but Isaiah through the prophet about how it was okay for Isaiah to get close to me and lay on me. When I heard that I took it as God was allowing Isaiah in my space. So while he was rubbing my arm I started to rub his head, but I shouldn't have done that because it felt good and the temptation was getting stronger. So we prayed about the situation and asked God to remove the spirit and take control of the situation.

It didn't go as planned and we ended up kissing. Then it turned into neck kisses which turned into feelings for each other. At that moment I never felt so aroused before. Isaiah and I had conversations about God and how our focus is on Him. Many don't know this, but there's nothing like a good conversation and a man that is chasing after God. Eventually while we were in the bed together that night we gave in and got intimate. That wasn't the last time either. We were going through trials every night we slept together.

When Craig left the shelter I felt more confident and free. I started opening up to my children about how Isaiah and I were dating. Truth be told they weren't very enthused by it at all. My son Sean wasn't too happy about that and he stopped talking to Isaiah for a while. My daughter Angel said she was okay with it because she saw how we needed each other, but she also thought it was for a season. She knew what Isaiah was going through at the time and what I was going through with Craig. Eventually when she started seeing my relationship with Isaiah was being built on fertile ground she began to get salty.

Even my youngest son Adrian showed that he was on board, but he missed his father, so he was wavering as well. The only child of mine that didn't say anything about it was my oldest son Damonte, and that was because he didn't know at all. He wasn't at the shelter because he felt ashamed. Isaiah didn't let it bother him much about how the kids felt, but I knew he felt some type of way. His biological family basically loved him, but chose to do it from a distance. What kept both of us from being discouraged about how my children reacted was understanding that God ordained it to happen.

Even then I kept doubting it myself because the way it looked and sounded seemed impossible from an outside view. Even when I was getting that revelation that God was connecting Isaiah and me to be, I rejected it and felt ashamed. I was pushing Isaiah off and attempting to throw him in the direction of other girls. I asked God myself if I was supposed to be with Isaiah. I asked Isaiah more times than I can count if he was sure that God ordained us to be together and how did he know for sure.

Sometimes I felt like he was just saying yes just because, but I also saw how confident Isaiah was when he told me that we were meant to be. Call me crazy, but when he talked I believed him. I felt insecure because of our age difference. He looked way younger than me, but when I say that I mean he had a baby face and was wet behind the ears. All in all to this day it worked for both of our good!

CHAPTER 17
Keonna Got Her Groove Back

I'm glowing! I can not believe I am this happy! Lord, is this real? If not, show me why this young man makes me feel like Stella got her groove back because I'm loving it. I have never felt this way before! The way Zay expresses himself when he speaks, when we're having conversations about making sure I'm ok and not ever wanting to see me hurt again, that warms my heart.

At the time I was going through my separation from Craig and things were happening rapidly. I was stepping into another dimension, something I never thought I would be going through. I was taking a leap of faith into the unknown! I was stepping into unfamiliar territory. The way Isaiah talks about God with me, how we pray and study together, that's everything I was looking for from my husband.

But with Craig, I asked and prayed to God plenty of times on his behalf that Craig would wake up and grow with me. I craved that because I knew I wanted to go deeper with God! The part that I cried about the most wasn't Craig, I cried because all of the things I wanted from Craig are in Zay. I prayed for a true man of God, someone I could have deep conversations with about God, someone who could encourage me, someone I could laugh and smile with. I'm talking about a man who is running towards God.

We had conversations about our future in God's will, how many kids Zay wanted, what our dreams and aspirations were. I can't explain it, all I know is I did not and I repeat *did not* have these feelings before. It's like someone sprinkled me with fairy dust. He knows when to hold me, how to love me, how to listen, how to pray for me and my children, showing them a great example of what a man should do. So yes, I'm sorry I can't take it back and I'm glad because whatever this is, it is very comforting. Zay is showing me the type of real man that I need!

Zay also is learning what he is looking for in a woman. Zay told me, "I'm not looking anymore. I found her, (referring to me). You were in my face the whole time." People are gonna have to deal with it because God ain't tell me no. We all know some of my children have a problem with it, but I already knew that would happen, and that's where I have a problem. I don't want anything to come between me and my kids, so it's affecting me. The ink ain't even dry on the divorce papers. There's a lot going on, but still I'm glowing.

I asked Sean why he couldn't be happy for me. I put everyone else before myself and I was already in a marriage, but I wasn't happy anymore. I was getting mistreated, not getting help with the bills, Craig wasn't spending time with the kids, not getting up as much as he should, not taking me out on dates, it was always the same ole same ole. I could never be myself. I always had to watch what I said. He was the jealous type. Hell, I couldn't even do my Bible study teachings without him getting under my post because one of his friends commented under it. He started talking to him disrespectfully, which was so embarrassing.

One time I was in church during praise and worship standing up and he was sitting down. I lifted my hands up to God and he hurried and grabbed my hand. Y'all know what I did? I snatched my hand from him with quickness. I told him, "Don't do that! Don't ever interrupt me when I'm giving my God His praise!" I don't know what spirit he was under, but I was not having that. So yes, if you see me happy, please don't judge me. I do enough of that by myself! Thank you, Zayiah, for going above and beyond for me and loving me through my toughest times.

Everyone knows I married Craig three times, not one divorce until now, and I have the Lord to thank for allowing me to have Isaiah to be my help in this season I'm in. Can't wait to see what's next!

CHAPTER 18
Birthday Trippin'

My birthday weekend started with my sister Bella calling me to check on how I was doing because she's been down this road before with a divorce. Bella knew that I was going through the most; I was on an emotional roller coaster. I cried and I cried as I looked at pictures of Craig and me. I didn't cry because I missed him, it was because I was angry. I'm so mad he didn't fight for our marriage. I'm so mad he wasn't obedient to what God was telling him to do. As I said earlier, obedience is greater than sacrifice. Everything

I ever wanted was with him, but I guess I wasn't the one for Craig.

So Bella called me up and asked, "What are you doing for your birthday?" I told her, "I don't know. I'm down for whatever. I'm single now... not ready to mingle but ready to enjoy my life." So she asked, "Would you like to go to New Orleans for your birthday? My treat!" I was excited. I had never been to New Orleans, so I told her, "I'm down!" I immediately went to the mall to get some outfits for my birthday weekend. On January 27, 2021, I had a phone call from Ms. E, my housing specialist. She asked me, "Keonna, are you packed?" I said, "Yes, why?" Ms. Ed replied, "You got the house!" I was ecstatic! I told her I didn't care that we were in a pandemic, I was going to squeeze her so tight to say thank you.

I appreciated her so much for everything she had done. I shouted, "Thank you!" to the Lord. Ms. E replied, "Keonna, it was your faith that got you the house. You kept turning down every house that I tried to get you in. Now don't you move no more! I had turned down houses that were in SE and SW DC that were close to where I did not want to be. I just couldn't deal with the people in those areas anymore. I wanted better for my family and myself. The Lord said not to compromise! We had been homeless for four months, so hearing that news was the best birthday gift ever. I will never forget that day!

The next day was my birthday and I was heading to New Orleans; it would be a new experience for me. When I got off of work my children threw me a surprise birthday party before I had to board my flight the next morning. I was so happy we had the party in a shelter and I had a surprise waiting for me. I got to see my grandbaby for my birthday. That was my second gift from God. Isaiah planned the party all by himself. He got the money for the party by doing doordash on a bicycle. I'm talking about whether it was snowing, raining or windy. He did what he felt he had to do. Isaiah gave some money to Angel so she can get something to make sure my birthday was special. By hearing and seeing all of what Isaiah did for me it showed me that he was a go-getter. God was and still is being so good to me through the storm.

I took so many pictures with my grandbaby because the way her mother was, I didn't know when I was gonna see her again. But then again, I knew I would see her soon because I was praying for it. The next day I was ready to go; I had packed the night before. Isaiah was the only one going with me to the airport. He wanted to make sure my phone was working before I left, so we went to MetroPCS to get my phone fixed.

I parked the car in front of the shelter and called an Uber to take us to the airport. When we arrived we went to get something to eat from Chick-fil-A and 20 minutes later I walked through the gate. My sister was meeting me at the airport in New Orleans, so I was on my own until then. I had my Louis Vuitton bag with me on the plane. I'd had that bag for a long time and as soon as I arrived in New Orleans my bag decided to pop! I was a little in shock, not because of the bag, but because of how it happened. I said, "Hold on, Lord, what is going on here?"

I had to wait at the airport for two more hours for my sister Bella and her friend to touch down. While I was waiting I went to the gift shop and looked around. They had so much stuff that had luck involved. I don't believe in luck, I'm only walking by faith and not by sight. Then I saw little voodoo dolls in the shop too, and it was creeping me out! They had devil socks in the gift shop and voodoo dolls in a cake. The instructions said you had to eat the cake all up until you found the voodoo doll. I think not! I thought, *Let me slide out of here and find something to eat!*

I went to the first hotdog place I came to. I forget the name of it, but a police officer who worked inside allowed me to stay there for two hours until my sister got off the plane with her best friend. From the looks of it her friend was cool. She liked taking pictures like me. Every five minutes she wanted to flick it up. We went to get a rental car and we drove off into the nightlife.

We arrived at our hotel on the strip where the scenery was lit, the music in the streets was playing, people were walking and enjoying the nightlife. As soon as we got to the strip, my sister got a guy to get us some weed even though we already had some. We went to a shop where they sell alcohol, cigars and everything there. The music was jammin' in front of the store so we posted up right there after we got permission from the store owner. My sister Bella thanked him for allowing us to chill right there in front of the store and smoke without trouble.

The guy that worked at the store was cool. I believe he was bisexual, not to judge or anything. I just love people that have fun. He wanted to hang out with us after he got off work at 11 p.m. He met us at the restaurant where we went to eat.

Near the restaurant we took pictures on the New Orleans streets in different locations. Man, we ate some of the best food they had, there was so much flavor bursting out, it was ridiculous. I would definitely go back just for their delicious food. The service was also good at the restaurant. While we were in the restaurant God allowed me to minister to my sister's best friend.

As I was ministering to her I started feeling negative energy around me. There was one particular guy staring at me as I was talking about Jesus. I really was not talking loud; it was like he had to really be ear hustling. It was like they could identify that God's children were in the building. Then people from other tables started looking at us like we didn't belong there. I just told myself, *Yeah, yeah! We are cute or whatever!*

Then me and the guy that was with us from the store started side chatting to each other. It was like we were the only ones in the room and no one could hear us. We were so in tune with the conversation on a spiritual level. He started telling me about myself, it was a little creepy, but I did recognize that he was a prophet. He told me that I take on so much from the people around me, and I never have time for myself. I asked him, "How do you know that?" He replied, "I can feel your energy, and it's good energy." He asked me, "Where have you been all my life?"

My sister Bella and her friend were talking and said, "Keonna has been saying since we got in here there's been negative energy. It's time for us to go!" The guy I was chatting with at the table said to them, "You should listen to her because she knows what she's talking about. She sees stuff that you all cannot see!" In my head I'm like how in the world does he know that! Then the nosey man that was eyeballing me all that night and ear hustling decided to come over to our table. He knew who I was for sure, I knew when I got home I had to do some more research because I refuse to not know who I am. It was bothering me that someone else knew me better than I knew myself.

I knew I didn't belong there, and he started to speak demonically towards me but I noticed that I was not afraid. I asked him if I could pray for him. He told me, "Don't pray for me; you better not." He kept getting close to me to the point he grazed my leg. I'm telling you, by the power of Jesus Christ I told him, "Move!" He literally glided across the room to another table. It was time to get out of there. My sister Bella and I got all of our belongings and left the restaurant. We went on another strip to take pictures.

While we were taking pictures, I noticed my bag wasn't on the ground in the place where I had put it originally. Mind you there was only a homeless man on the strip sleeping and the guy that had been with us all night. He was on the phone taking our pictures but really my pictures! Just like that my purse went missing along with my food. That was really creepy because I was only taking pictures for 5 minutes. Maybe it caught me off guard because I was high. It was like some voodoo magic. We looked through the pictures, we walked around the streets, and we still found no purse. I didn't get upset, I was just worried about getting back on the plane. I had my credit and bank cards in my purse.

We went back to the hotel and I checked to see if I had anything that would get me home. I had my backup drivers license and $110 in cash for emergencies. I'm telling you it ain't nothing but God. The enemy had to do something because I was still on assignment on my trip. My sister told me, "Don't even worry about it." We got on the phone immediately and canceled all of my cards. It was a little frustrating but I got it done, to God be the glory!

The next day we left the hotel and went to the airport. We got something to eat before my sister and Pearl had to board their flight. I had to wait until 5 p.m. to board my flight back to Washington. When it was finally time to board, it was still daylight on my end in New Orleans. I never got to see the sky at night while on the plane, so I was intrigued. With that being said, I stayed by the window.

As I looked outside the window, I saw a flash of light. It was so bright I couldn't miss it. It was roaming the earth and I made sure it wasn't from the plane. I believe it was an angel roaming the earth, making sure everything was okay and in order. The angel followed me all the way home. I thank you, Lord, for your divine protection and for always showing me signs and wonders. Amen. I took an Uber to the shelter after I got to the airport. The next day was packing day for the Young family, so I had to get rest the night before. I was so excited!

I was still unsettled about my relationship with Isaiah, so I prayed to God and asked him to remove the feelings I had for Isaiah and let it go back to a mother and son connection. I didn't wanna be with him, and I didn't wanna hurt him. Later on the next day Isaiah told me that he didn't think he was supposed to be filling out the divorce papers for me. He said it was because every time he tried to do it, it never worked out for him and he thought that was a sign. I told him he was probably right; maybe I was supposed to be doing it myself. It just wasn't time to do it yet; I had too much to focus on.

He also said he thought God had been telling him that we can't be together anymore because I was still married. I told him, "Right, I agree." Then I said, "Dang, Zay, you breaking up with me?" But in all actuality I asked God to do that, so if he broke up with me it wouldn't hurt me. But I was worried if *I* did it to him it may crush him. I didn't wanna hurt his feelings, so thank you, Lord!

CHAPTER 19
Sean's Family Tree

It was a special day. I took my son Sean to see his father's side of the family. I'm not sure if I told you guys, but Sean has a different father than my other children. It was so important to him knowing where he came from, he had Craig to thank for that. Craig was always bringing it up in arguments and stating the obvious that I had a child by someone else. Sean getting to know his family was important and would play a part later in his life. I knew that if he got to know his sisters and brothers, he wouldn't have to worry about dating his sisters in the future. That's incest!

When we went over there to meet Sean's family he was able to meet his grandmother and aunt. His aunt asked me, "Why didn't you bring him around a long time ago? We missed sixteen years of his life." I told her I gave Tye the opportunity to do that when my son was six years old. I told Tye, "If you want to be in your child's life, let me know. Don't wait until my husband comes around to start trouble." But Tye did the very thing I asked him not to do. I think he likes drama. I told Sean's aunt that she would have to take that up with Tye. The ball was in his court.

I also reached out to Sean's grandma and asked her if she wanted to see him. She said she did, but it never happened. I guess life got in the way. I wasn't going to call and press her on it, after all, she had a lot of Tye's kids. He not only made Sean, he also fathered six others, if not more, so I believe I did the right thing by letting them meet. Sean got to see one of his sisters. She was thirteen years old and was happy to see him. I love taking pictures, so I had to capture the moment.

Not thinking anything of it and with all good intentions, I wanted to share the good news with my family and friends on Facebook. I added some of Sean's family to my Friends list so we could keep in touch. To my surprise I got a phone call from you know who...the big bad wolf, Craig. "Keonna, so I'm not Sean's father? I heard you got a post up," Craig said. Yes, I have him blocked.

Craig is nothing but trouble on my page if I put a post up. It's like competition to him, but I ain't for that. Craig still wanted to yap. He said, "So you took him to see his dad. That's how we are going?" I replied, "First of all he did not see his father! Sean wanted to meet his grandma and siblings, but everyone wasn't available to meet. So please don't make it about you. This is about Sean and what he wants. That's what matters to me!"

I had to hang up on Craig because he was going off yelling. He was upset about it and since I didn't want to get upset with him, the call had to end. I told my daughter Angel, "Don't give me the phone for him again, please!" I knew I had blocked him on social media, so one of his family members had to be all in it. Then Lisha told me it was his mom that told him. I couldn't understand that because she knew that he would go off and probably try to do something to me physically – but God.

Later on that day I got a horrible phone call from Lisha saying, "Craig is missing. Have you heard from him after y'all got off the phone with each other?" I told her no, and that was the truth. The last time I talked to Craig was around 5:30, close to 6. I knew the time because I was headed to church on a Saturday because my pastor wanted my family and I there so he wouldn't have to preach to empty chairs. The news had called for snow on Sunday, so he streamed the church service on Saturday for Sunday.

Lisha told me Craig was with his cousin Aaron and they went in a cab around Southeast to get his mind off of what was going on with me and him. I told Lisha, "First of all Craig doesn't even belong around Southeast. When will enough be enough?" God had told him to stay away from people, places and things! Craig had a strong bond with family and friends. He loved being outside and always had loyalty to the wrong people. That loyalty caused Craig to make poor choices. Craig also loved getting high and people knew his drug of choice. You know that saying, "Birds of a feather flock together." So yeah, they knew.

I always tried to talk to each of them and tell them, "One of you has to leave the flock and come back as an example." I was definitely praying that it would be Craig because I knew if I didn't do anything else, I had to make sure I planted the seed! The drug of choice was called a dipper, which was embalming fluid for dead bodies. It surely made him feel alive and strong. I'm telling you, he wouldn't feel a thing if something happened to him while he was on that drug.

Craig really has been through a lot and put me through a lot! Lisha said their other cousin had called her and asked, "Is Craig on any drugs?" Lisha asked, "Why?" The cousin replied, "From what I saw he lunched out, then pushed me and ran off by ManMan's house." Lisha's sister called her and she said she saw a lot of blood in front of her apartment building. I immediately went into prayer for Craig and covered him because I didn't want anything to happen to him even though we broke up.

I still have love for him. We have only been together forever. You can't just cut that off; I would be faking if I said I could. I want our separation to bring the best out in him and me. I figured if we'd let each other go, we would get the lesson and grow from the mistakes we made in the past. I want what God has for me!

I received a phone call from Craig later on that day and he said, "I got stabbed up and I'm in George Washington Hospital." I asked him if he knew who did it, but Craig said he didn't know. *SMH...*

I called Lisha back and told her he had contacted me. I told her where he was and told her I wasn't going up there this time. I would usually run when Craig got hurt, but that's what he knows: Keonna is gonna come no matter what he does. I had to stand my ground, I had to get out of the cycle. I saw myself continuing to go around and around, but I knew this time had to be different! I really couldn't go even if I wanted to. Due to COVID-19, no one could go into the hospital with the patient or even visit the patient.

Craig called me the next day and let me know what was going on. He told me again that he didn't even know what happened to him. For the life of me I just didn't understand him. I asked him, "When is enough gonna be enough? Why don't you know what happened to you? It happened to you!" Craig told me, "Stink, I don't know. The doctor said I got stabbed around 23 times. I'm sorry." That's what he always says; he thinks he is a cat and has nine lives. I think he is already at seven if not more!

I had to tell my children what happened to their father. They shook their heads and sometimes cried. They were trying to figure out the same thing. Craig has a rock head! I took my daughter Angel and Adrian to see their dad Craig when he got out of the hospital. He went to Lisha's house and we met him there. I didn't wanna go, but I needed to go to pray over him. That's all I wanted to do and to make sure he was okay. That didn't go as planned.

His cousin Timmy was there and he was asking me questions about my marriage. Timmy didn't have any right to speak about our marriage. Craig just stood there letting him keep saying reckless stuff to me. I know what y'all are thinking, *What did you want him to do? He just got stabbed up.* Yeah, but he allows things like this anyway, regardless. That's the point I was trying to make!

I told my husband, "You got to get away from people, places and things that don't mean you no good. Just because they're family doesn't mean anything! I really believe your cousin had something to do with you getting stabbed. So you need to be careful who you hang around! I always told you that if you don't listen to anything else I say, listen to this!"

Craig's cousin Timmy asked, "What church do you go to?" My face immediately started to frown and I asked, "Why?" His cousin Timmy said, "Because why would a church tell you to leave your husband?" I immediately responded, "First of all, why are you in my business? Second, no church told me to leave my husband." I looked over at Craig and said, "Craig, I hope you ain't telling him to run people away from church." I told Craig to tell him who told me that! Craig responded, "I don't know, you said God told you, but I don't think God told you that!"

Soon we were going back and forth. I was not only going back and forth with my husband but with his cousin Timmy too. Not to mention Lisha that I do everything with was just as quiet as a mouse. One thing

I noticed, when you're salty you can't help but be quiet. It shows how strong the friendship really is!

I didn't want to disrespect Lisha's home and I didn't want the drama anymore, so I told Craig, "You got everybody in our business and let your cousin say whatever he wants to me. I realize, Craig, you never had my back against nobody, not your family or friends. I always had to have my own back and that was fine. I have God. I'm covered, I know who I belong to!" When it was time for Craig to speak up for me, he didn't. He was basically still saying, *F**k your feelings.*

I hurried up and smoked a jay to clear my mind and calm down from all of the bull s**t. Life can be cruel and break you into pieces, but it's how you pick them up and give the pieces you have to God and allow Him to sort them out so God can use them to create a beautiful masterpiece and stay blessed!

CHAPTER 20
Move-in Day

Yay, we're moving out of the shelter and moving into a new house. The landlord was taking forever to give us the keys. I had to call Ms. E and tell her what was going on. I asked Ms. E, "When will we be able to pick up the keys for our new house?" Ms. E told me it was taking longer than expected and that they were waiting for some paperwork to be done. The landlord had to sign the lease.

It took the landlord till 7 o'clock that night to give us the keys to our new home and the shelter manager said she would not be able to move us until the next day. We had the keycard to the shelter rooms and the keys to the house. We didn't want to wait it out any longer, so we took it in our own hands and packed my van and made three trips. When we were done we gave the shelter their keycards back and told them we appreciated everything they had done for us. I took the rest of us back to the house, but I had to go to work the same night. I left them in the house to unpack some of the things and put them where they belonged.

The next day Ms.Mya met us at the U-Haul place and paid for a U-Haul for us to get the rest of our stuff from storage and my dad's house. I had to drive a 26 foot U-Haul, which was the biggest one! I actually don't have any issue with driving big trucks; it comes natural to me. We only had the truck for 4 hours, so we had to keep things moving, not to mention it was snowing sticks and carrots.

After getting all of our stuff from the storage unit, there was only an hour left, but we still had to go to my dad's house. I called my dad and told him that we were at the house, but he wasn't there. I asked him when he was coming home And he said he was on his way. When he finally got there we got our belongings from his house and he decided to go with us. I was shocked and happy because my dad doesn't really go anywhere. My dad was so excited that he helped us move stuff on and off the truck because he used to do that as a job when he was younger.

My dad hadn't driven in like nine years, but he decided to help me get out of a narrow alley that's in the back of his apartment because we were stuck. That didn't go well, and I noticed then just how hard headed my dad was. I was trying to tell him that he was about to hit the back of the wall. He was too close and I was telling him to stop. My dad didn't listen nor did the other person that was trying to help direct us. I just told my dad to get out of the truck and I would do it. So the guys helped me out while I backed the truck up out of the alley.

My dad was upset. He said I didn't listen to him, but in actuality he wasn't listening to me. After all of that mess, we had to unload the things off the truck at my house. It was a small street and we had that big truck. While we were organizing and unpacking, someone was beeping the horn in the street to get us to move the truck. My dad said he'd go do it. I told him no, but he did it anyway.

My dad was so excited to move the truck he jumped in without hesitation. He moved the truck a little for the car to get by, but he had to put it in reverse to get the truck back into the position it was in previously. While he was getting it back into position, he kept backing up unnecessarily, and for the life of me I don't know why.

I told Damonte to hurry up and tell him he's too close to the car. Adrian was even out there waving his hands to signal him to stop while yelling it. My dad acted like he didn't see anything or hear anything, he backed up too far and crushed my neighbor's cab. The devil is a liar! The bumper was completely totaled.

My dad got out of the car, looked at the damage and tried to say he couldn't hear or see anything because the radio was too loud. When he came inside the house I said, "Dad… why? The neighbors saw us moving in and that is not how you want to introduce yourself to the neighborhood." He responded, "I was trying to get close to the cars so I wouldn't be in the middle of the street." My dad was acting so nonchalant like everything was okay and nothing had happened. He told me, "Just tell the U-Haul people that you were driving and you made a mistake."

I could not believe my dad was saying this out of his mouth, not to mention with a smirk on his face. I said, "So you want me to lie and I didn't even do it? *You* did it!" At that point I just couldn't take any more of it. It was like the enemy just kept coming at me and using all of the people I love the most to come against me. I had to ask the Lord, "Am I doing something wrong?"

That night I went to my new bedroom and I felt some negative energy above my bed. It was coming from the attic and I'm telling y'all it was really bad. That energy was not staying in my bedroom, let alone my house, so I told Isaiah we had to pray and we had to open all of the windows in the entire house. Trust me, you don't just wanna pray in the room it's in because all it will do is transfer to another spot in the house. We prayed and commanded the spirits to leave, in the name of Jesus.

How many of you know there is power in the name of Jesus? I had to go to work the same night, so I told them to leave the windows open all night. I hurried up and jumped in the shower because it was time for me to go to work. I had to wash my hair and my body to get the evil spirits away. I didn't have time to dry my hair, so I just put a towel around it and left the house. The next morning I woke up with a cold. My nose was leaking and I couldn't breathe. My body felt drained.

I immediately lay back down in the bed and Isaiah made me soup, gave me some tea, and I took some DayQuil to get better. On the second day of being sick, I started to feel a change. Thank you, Jesus, I felt much better. I'm really blessed to have the house He gave me. As I walked around in it, I was taking it all in. God blessed my family and me, which makes me wanna praise Him more, do more for the Kingdom and His people, like He has done for us. I love Jesus! I just want to do better for myself.

Looking at the house God blessed me with, it also had me inspired to do some decorating. I love to decorate! I didn't ever get to decorate my other homes. Craig always said we couldn't afford it, it wasn't ever in our budget, but weed, cigarettes, liquor and going out was in our budget? Craig's favorite line was to wait until we got more money. Looking back on the situation, I can't believe I really allowed someone that didn't have money tell me what to do with mine. I thank God I don't have to worry about that anymore! I get to express myself how I want to; I'm finally getting to see Keonna in a different light.

I was so used to doing things a certain way and when you don't know who you are it's scary. I'm in the process of finding out who Keonna is and what she likes and doesn't like, glory to God. I am so embarrassed to say it, but I need to tell people the truth. I just wanna encourage you and let you know that everything is going to be okay. Just make sure you put your faith in God alone and be obedient. I'm so excited to be on this journey with God, figuring out who Keonna is and what Keonna is supposed to be doing in life.

I do know what makes Keonna happy and that is helping others know Jesus. Being the salt in the earth is not easy, but it's necessary! Whatever the enemy tries to tell you, come against it and know God made us the head and not the tail, above and not beneath, the lender and not the borrower. Stay blessed, family, and keep pressing towards greatness! Remember there is power in the name of Jesus!

CHAPTER 21
Valentine's Where?

It was another Valentine's Day, but I really couldn't get excited about it. I knew I shouldn't feel like that, but I never really felt special on Valentine's Day because nothing romantic was ever planned. Craig wasn't thoughtful about that day at all. He would ask me what I wanted to do on Valentine's Day. That's the most unthoughtful thing you can do.

He could've asked God what he should do to make his wife feel special and loved. Why would you wait until

Valentine's Day to plan what to do when it's on the same day every year? Why not plan ahead?

He gave me heartfelt Valentine's Day cards and flowers, which I loved, but that was pretty much it. At the end of the day I always ended up crying and arguing with him over dumb stuff, all because I wanted to feel special. My son Sean woke me up with flowers and a stuffed animal turtle with chocolates on it. I love turtles because God showed me turtles are my spiritual animal, and it reminds me slow and steady wins the race. I felt it was very thoughtful for him to buy that gift. Sean also gave me a card. One side of the card said, You taught me that love is gracious and kind, strong and brave and stops at nothing. The other side said, Especially on Valentine's Day. I want to thank you for being the first person to teach me about love and the first person to have her own place in my heart.

Sean was excited about Valentine's Day because he had a date with his girlfriend. After we got ourselves together and fresh, we put the GPS on and headed to his girlfriend's house, but we went the wrong way for 30 minutes; can you believe it? When we got close enough to her house we stopped at the gas station and

I let him brush up on his driving skills for the last five minutes to his girlfriend's house. I gave him precise instructions on what to do. I don't have to worry about Sean when it comes to driving. He listens very well and I feel safe when he drives me around. When we pulled up to her house, Sean gave her flowers, candy and a card. They were so cute together. My son expresses his affection in his relationship, I was proud.

I grabbed my phone and got in mommy mode and took lots of photos while they were hugged up. LOL. I had a missed call from Craig while taking pictures, so before I got back on the road I returned the call. He was fussing because he thought I was getting out of his life. I was told by God through a pastor, "Stop opening doors that I closed!" But I began talking on the phone with Craig after that.

See, in one ear I had people telling me to go back for Craig, to stay with my husband, but the message was clear as day through that pastor that I have never met. I just knew God told me what I should've been doing for Craig from the beginning, basically just praying and giving him the word of God and allowing Him to be God in Craig's life. I blocked Craig when I first realized God told me I was free and to part ways from him. Yes, there were a lot of emotions and feelings I was going through. I really did love Craig, and all I ever wanted was for him to do better and be the kingdom man God called him to be and lead by example.

I wanted Craig to support me in anything I did and support his family, be a provider, an equal partner, be romantic, be desirable and worthy of the love that I had to give. Most importantly my prayer was for whomever I was supposed to be with would have love for Jesus and follow Him and His teachings, and that I would have everything I asked for in a man because the good Lord would be leading him. After I got off the phone with Craig I headed home.

Once I got home, Isaiah kept coming upstairs to my room. He is an affectionate person and very clingy. I was a little afraid of it at first. I never had someone that really wanted to be around me without drugs and drinking. I'm still like Sarah in the Bible looking back when God is trying to move me forward in another direction, SMH. I wanted to talk to Craig on the phone again, but Zay was right there. I kept pushing him away because of all the reasons that came in my head to makc me say, *Yeah... um, no!* I realized I really missed my husband so much, but he still was not right, still choosing the streets and not me. I felt stupid every time I missed him, but he blatantly was showing me he couldn't care less.

My heart still skips a beat for him. Lord, please protect my heart, don't let me go backwards. After I got Zay out of my room I talked to Craig and he wanted to see me, so I drove to Lisha's house. He came outside when I pulled up. I didn't want to go inside Lisha's house because of the many spirits in there. He came in my van and turned on slow music, songs that I didn't even know he knew. Crazy thing, the whole time we were married he never did that, but once we were apart, I guess he realized he should've been doing it all along (lessons).

Craig took me out of the car and we danced. Anybody that knows Craig knows he doesn't dance, LOL. People were beeping the horn at us and waving. At that point it didn't matter about a gift or anything else, I just felt loved!

It was time for me to go so we kissed and I headed home. When I FaceTimed him later Craig said he got me a gift, but I had to come and get it. I'd just left there like 3 hours ago, but when I arrived, I knew that look. I'd seen it plenty of times before – he looked high! I couldn't believe it. I cried my little eyes out. All of the ministering to him in hopes of us getting back and staying together was soon fading away before my eyes. You see, I learned when God tells you to do something, do it. It's for your protection.

Obedience is key; you cannot follow God and your emotions. Look where mine got me – nowhere. But I did get another lesson and gained wisdom. He kept calling me to try and plead his case, but I really wasn't mad, I was more so hurt by his choices. When people show you with their actions you cannot add to it by masking it to fit your way. This is not Burger King stuff. That's important to me, but it seemed to be less important to him, at least that's what he showed me through his actions.

Craig asked me not to give up on him. I won't. I will continue to pray to my Father on his behalf because that's what love does. Craig wanted me to continue to text him. I replied with, "OK, I don't feel like being bothered at the moment. Please give me my space." If I hadn't said that to Craig, he would have kept blowing my phone up and I didn't want that. I need peace, you feel me?

Craig called my phone and asked if I was coming over to visit sometime that day. I told him I would think about it. I didn't know if I was supposed to go see him all the time, and why should I? All he had to do was do what God had told him to and he would still be in the house with his family! I wasn't sure if I was supposed to be visiting with him. I had to focus on my own things that I had going on and figuring out what God wanted me to do. I ended up telling Craig to call me a little later. When Craig called me back I told him, "I can't get over us, I've been horny and I'm going through things."

Craig said, "You should come over here." I said, "I should, I already had to throw away my dildo, but I'm tired." Craig said, "Get some rest, love." I got off the phone with him and I thought I was headed to sleep, but it didn't happen. I got hungry so I asked Zayiah if he would make me some breakfast and he said, "Yes." After Zayiah finished making breakfast, I ate before I decided to jump in the shower and get dressed. After I finished getting freshened up I was on my way to Craig.

Craig told me he was just leaving to go to MetroPCS to figure out what was wrong with his phone. It's obvious to me he had a side agenda because since I had a car why wouldn't he ask me to take him instead of walking. I asked him which MetroPCS store he was going to. He told me he was heading to Landover because that was the only MetroPCS he was close enough to walk to. *Hmmm... yeah right!* That was his hangout spot! I had just told Craig about how God wants him away from people, places and things, but clearly he still didn't get it. That was a sign right there, but I bypassed it like usual.

When I got to Lisha's house Craig came outside. I asked him, "Where is the Bible and journal I bought you?" Look y'all, the enemy uses anything, by any means necessary, even the word of God to throw you off your course. The Bible does say something like leave the 99 and go back for that one. In this case I figured that's what I was supposed to do; after all, I did love him. When I saw that he didn't bring his Bible or journal outside, I took that as another sign that he wasn't really about the word, he was more focused on the "I'm horny" part!

Craig got back out of the car and went to get his Bible and journal from Lisha's house where he still lived for the time being.

When he came back out he told me he started reading the book of Deuteronomy. I was trying to figure out why he was in the Old Testament and not the New Testament because the New Testament is the covenant that God gave us to live by. I knew Craig didn't quite understand what he was reading, so I decided to help him out. Let me explain what my motive was behind going back "For that one."

I was doing one-on-one Bible studies with Craig. We were reading scriptures and we would try to break it down together. I was reading his flashcards with scriptures on them to help him memorize the promises of God whenever he goes through something. But before I or anyone I am with starts studying the Bible, Rule Number 1: Pray First! I asked Craig, "Why am I holding your hand?" Craig was still a little lost. I asked Craig, "What did I tell you yesterday?" Craig looked at me puzzled and high. I should've known he was high when he was going, "Out to MetroPCS to see what was wrong with his phone."

I told him again, "We are always supposed to be praying before we do anything. That's what a great leader does." Crazy part is out of all of the stuff that Craig put me through, I still wanted to help him. After we finished doing Bible study we smoked a white boy and listened to some slow jams. (Yes, I was smoking due to my trauma from my surgery that caused nerve damage.) Craig was so used to playing trap music I didn't even know he knew slow songs. It's amazing how when you separate from someone they start to notice what they lost or what they should've been doing in the first place.

"Pull up around the back of Lisha's house," Craig said. I asked him, "For what?" He said, "You know what you told me." I said, "You know what... I don't know about that." He said again, "Pull up around the back." I pulled up around back and it was still daylight so we chilled until it got dark. He decided to go in the back seat and told me, "Let me handle that for you." I went to the back seat with him and we started kissing. When I kissed him his breath, his tongue and his mouth tasted like water (embalming fluid). I had already asked him if he had smoked that stuff. Craig said, "No," which I now knew was a bold faced lie!

I knew that was a sign that it was time to get out of that situation. Craig was still lying so I changed my mind and told him, "I don't think we should do this." He grabbed me so tight. He said he was not letting me go because I had already told him I wanted it, so he was gonna give it to me. Craig didn't want me to get it from anywhere else, so he was not gonna let me go until I let him get some action.

I pulled my pants down and let him do it, man... I was on my period and he didn't care. He usually says, "Let me lick the tip," but this time he just went all in. It was good. He made sure he put that snap in his neck, but I was upset with myself because I kept letting myself get in the situation again and again. I knew that I had to get out of there, but then he started crying and pleading his case. He knew I wasn't feeling it. He knew that I was trying to get away from that whole situation.

Craig said, "Stink, please don't give up on me, don't give up on me yet! Please, if I quit this drug right now, take me back! Please! Just take me and I quit the drug." I told him, "It's not up to me. It's up to God!" Craig wasn't trying to hear that. So I pulled up around front, I told him I had to leave and he got out of the car. He gave me a kiss and said, "Please, don't do this to me." I told him, "I'll talk to God about it and get back with you."

I rushed home because it was almost 8 o'clock. It was almost time for me to chat with Pastor V on Zoom. When I started chatting with her I was telling her that I listened to her sermon online. She was talking about going back for that one you are not showing love to. I told her I immediately thought of my husband. Pastor V waited until I finished telling her what I did, which was to go to Craig and help him with the Bible and all of that. She told me I was going in the wrong direction. She told me God wouldn't want me to go backwards when He is calling me higher. The blessings that He has in store for me are much better than what's being left behind. When she told me that I asked her, "Now that the door is open, what do I do?" I thought I was doomed, but Pastor V replied, "You have to close it back!"

After hearing that I knew what I had to do. It broke me down; it was worse than the first time. I texted my husband and told him I was sorry. I had to close the door that I opened. Craig told me he was never gonna give up or let go. When I got off the phone with Craig, I blocked him from social media. I just thank God for ordering my steps because I noticed when I was on the phone with Pastor V, she was telling me I needed to find myself. I needed to know more about what Keonna wanted, what Keonna liked and my dislikes. I needed to figure out what my purpose was.

Pastor V told me, "Keonna, you help everyone else, but who helps you?" Pastor V *nailed it!* She told me to go on a quest to unfamiliar places I have never been to do things I have never done. I made sure I talked to God along the way and diligently sought him (Jeremiah 29:11). From that point on I made sure I asked the Lord more than once before I made a move. It could've been worse. Thank God it wasn't!

CHAPTER 22
Exploring Me

Isaiah and I were sitting down having a conversation about God, life and where God is taking us. We agreed that we needed to be prepared for what's to come. We were engaged in our conversations so deep that emotions started to rise. I started crying because I realized how much emotional pain I'd been through. The thoughts in my head kept antagonizing me. Looking back at the stuff that I put up with from Craig, I couldn't believe I had lasted a long twenty-one years of my life with him.

I also felt sad because at the same time the Lord was showing me my faults in the relationship as well. I'll admit I wasn't praying for my husband enough nor going in the word to seek for the Lord's help. Instead of doing my wifely responsibilities, I chose to entertain the fleshly nature. When Isaiah started to uplift and encourage me by telling me how gorgeous and beautiful I am he made me feel special and loved. I felt comfortable about myself and around Isaiah.

I never showed my burn to anybody... until now. He knew what songs to play when I was feeling down, he knew how to make me laugh a little. There is no such thing as "The Perfect One" but there is a perfect one for me. As we continued to bond with each other Isaiah got familiar with me down to a T. He knows what to do to make me happy even though all of what I saw was starting to get to be a bit much because a part of me still looked at him as my son.

My favorite time with Isaiah is when we are reading the Bible and studying together, that's what I wanted to do with my husband. My prayers were being answered by God because I asked for a man to encourage me. I asked God for a man who wants to participate with me in praying and praising. I asked God to give me a man who I can open up to and he actually cares and listens to me. Especially a man who won't judge me or tear me down.

I got sick and tired of being sick and tired. God knows the heart and he paid attention to mine. When I surrendered to God that's when the healing process began. I uplift Isaiah and he uplifts me. Isaiah got rejected and carried all his life by girls. As for me I never had anyone uplift me or want to be there for me. I haven't had a husband who wants to pray for me and study the word with me like Isaiah. Isaiah is also very affectionate, I was the total opposite until I met Isaiah. God was using Isaiah to plant those seeds in me, especially 1 Corinthians 13.

Isaiah also mentioned to me that I was the first person that ever showed and told him his worth. I do think he is over the top with his affection, but it's very genuine. I didn't get hugs and kisses when I was growing up, so it seemed a bit much, but I thank God for Isaiah because now I am affectionate. I feel that everything happened for a reason. It was very purposeful! When you stay focused on the Lord, all things are possible to them that love the Lord and believe. "Ask, and it shall be given to you; seek, and ye shall find; knock, and it shall be opened unto you" (Matthew 7:7).

CHAPTER 23
Doubts and Convictions

In the middle of the year 2021, Isaiah and I began to get closer. The house was empty and that helped our feelings grow stronger for each other since there were fewer distractions. Sean and Adrian were staying over at their uncle's house. Angel was over her boyfriend's (now ex-boyfriend's) house. And Deonte was nowhere near the perimeter of the house.

Isaiah and I started giving in to our flesh by going at each other like rabbits. We were hugging each other for long periods of time just because and dancing with each other. We were laying on each other and then he would give me massages on my back, my feet and my butt. Like I said before, he knew what songs to play at the right time. When I was sad he would put on gospel songs like, "Still," and "In the Midst of It All." When I wasn't sad he would play artists like Anita Baker. He knows I love Anita. The name of our favorite song is "The Point of It All" by Anthony Hamilton.

I remember a time when we were sitting in the van and we were expressing our feelings to each other. Zayiah was saying how he believed God had us destined to be together for more than love – for purpose. A proper marriage does take a lot of work and responsibility. You should treat it like work, which should be done in excellence but not a job. There is a big difference!

Isaiah said he visualized a family with me. He also told me he really wants a daughter. Isaiah said he just wants everything to be right with God. I got my tubes tied not too long ago. I took Zayiah to the mirror of my room to see how we would look together. As I observed his smile with his dimple showing and his arms wrapped around me, it did look like we fit together. I asked Isaiah if he liked me because of my height? He said,

"Yes." He wasn't attracted to girls taller than him. I don't know why, but he doesn't have to worry about that anymore.

In my head I was starting to believe what Isaiah said to me was true. I asked God later on, "Please tell me what's going on and give me signs and clarity on the situation between Zayiah and me." I didn't get a response at that moment. Even though I wasn't fully aware at the time, I now know that when I ask God a question and I don't get a response that means I already have been told the answer.

Isaiah and I kept doing what we were doing. We were in the shower together, playing uplifting music. When Isaiah didn't get in the shower with me he would sit on the toilet and wait for me to finish. When I got out of the shower he would have a towel and robe ready for me. After we moved out of the bathroom he would rub me with oil or lotion all over my body to make sure I wasn't ashy. My favorite part about that was when he rubbed my feet, LOL.

Now after all of that rubbing, it was out of our control so you know what happened next! After that we went in the car and smoked. While we were in the car we were talking about how to stop having sex with each other. I told Isaiah, "I don't know if I'm the one for you, but we need to stop this because God already told both of us that we needed to stop." The steps we came up with were to set boundaries, like we'll just do bible study together and listen to the sermons.

While we were high in the car I looked in the rear view mirror and I confessed I don't like looking at myself when I'm high because that's not who I am. I immediately put in my Clear Eyes and prayed. I give the highest praise to God because He delivered me! Today and forevermore I am never getting hooked, enslaved or bound to a stupid demonic drug ever again! Faith pleases God.

The Lord says in Isaiah 41:10, "I will uphold you with My righteous right hand." God promises to uphold us. More than that, He promises to uphold us with His righteous right hand. That means when you lose your footing, He's going to be there to hold you up if you'll trust in Him. Regardless of your circumstances, God is righteous, just and faithful to us even when we don't deserve it.

CHAPTER 24
Warning Before Destruction

One morning we felt convicted by the Holy Spirit prior to things that took place between me and Zayiah the night before. The Holy Spirit is real! We knew we did something wrong and He definitely convicted us of it. I was separated from Craig, but still married to him. We came to an agreement to focus just on God and His word, not our needs! We tried our best to not be affectionate. It was very hard because Zayiah still wanted to hold and kiss my hand. Those were the things that we should have boundaries on.

After not giving in all day, finally night time came. It was almost time for me to go to work, so Zayiah and I decided to lay down in the bed and chill. Then Zayiah rubbed up on me and he started groping me. He kissed me and said, "I want you." I said, "Zayiah, you do? Are we doing a finale?" He replied, "Yes!" I pounced on him and it was on! After we were done I took a shower then I went to work.

I got home the next morning and I was anticipating the message from Breakfast of Champions at 8 a.m. That specific morning the pastor didn't come on at 8, which is her usual time. So I stayed on Facebook and watched another stream. Zayiah came up the steps from the basement with his laptop and we were on the stream at the same time the pastor started the live. I was feeling bad about the night before when we gave in and we promised God that we wouldn't do it again. So we repented and since we repented we would turn away from the wrong things we were doing that weren't pleasing in God's sight.

The pastor was talking about how we were in week 70 with no days off in the Breakfast of Champions. I felt the presence of God in my room while she was preaching about adultery and fornication. It was another confirmation that what we were doing needed to be stopped immediately! God started speaking about the wrath that He would bring on us. We would have Ishmael and not Isaac. He said that we would be producing bad fruit and we didn't want that. My kids already didn't like the idea of Zayiah being around me so much. I had to put my feelings aside because it was hurting my kids. When we asked them in the shelter how they felt about our relationship, they said they really didn't care, but that's not what we saw from them.

The pastor was saying those who remain in faith will be saved! She said, "Get saved and stay saved. You have to remain in position." She also said, "No answer is an answer." There's a reason for everything and a lesson in purpose. Today I can say Zayiah learned his value about knowing who he is in the Lord. He also learned not to let anyone tear him down. For my part, I learned how to be affectionate, which had been a major problem in my life with Craig

"But Samuel replied, 'What is more pleasing to the Lord: your burnt offerings and sacrifices or your obedience to his voice? Listen! Obedience is better than sacrifice, and submission is better than offering the fat of rams'" (1 Samuel 15:22).

CHAPTER 25
In and Out

Craig called me one day and asked to take me out on a date. I know I should've said no, but I hadn't been going out lately. I asked my daughter and her friend if they wanted to go with us because I didn't want to go by myself. They both said, "Yes. Who's paying?" I replied to Angel, "Your father." After I got some travel buddies we left to go pick up Craig from Licia's house. When I arrived at Licia's house to pick Craig up, he was already outside waiting. He didn't know I brought company with me, but I figured I would surprise him.

I got out of the car and gave him a hug. I realized he had smoked a dipper, which I had asked him not to do before I came. I was angry, but I still let him get in the car because I'm not his judge, but I also know the Holy Spirit will have his way! I'm also learning that I can't control everything, but I can control what I do and that's why I wasn't with him. I decided that since he couldn't do what I asked, I would run up the food bill.

While we were heading to the restaurant, the girls were listening to music and I was talking to Craig about using this time apart from me to get himself together. How he must get away from people, places and things that are not beneficial for him. I told him, "Just because they are family or close friends to you doesn't mean they have your best interest at heart."

Craig was talking about buying a car with money that he'd gotten from unemployment, and I stopped him in his tracks. I asked him to please reconsider buying a car. I asked him, " Craig, you don't see a pattern and the cycle you keep going through? Please don't get a car, especially if you are still smoking dippers. You already got high and crashed like four or five times and three of them could have taken your life. Why don't you ask God what your purpose is on earth? There's a reason He keeps sparing your life. Do you know why?" Craig said, "No I don't."

Craig always wanted me to have the answer for him instead of asking God about it. We all have the same power to speak openly to God. The veil was lifted when Jesus died on the cross and rose again on the third day. We all have the access to ask anything in Jesus' name. "And on that day ye shall ask me nothing. Verily, verily, I say unto you, Whatsoever ye shall ask the Father in my name, he will give it to you." (John 16:24)

After Craig told me that he didn't know his soul purpose, I told him he should go to rehab and get away from everybody and allow God to speak to him. Allow it to be just Craig and the Lord! While we were on our dinner date, Craig's phone kept going off. I found out it was a girl who kept blowing up his phone. Craig kept declining the call. I asked him why he wasn't answering the phone. He replied, "She can wait." It was a turn off for me, but hey, we were not together anyway. That further let me know that it was premeditated, and that Craig already had a backup or replacement in mind.

After the dinner we were in the car talking about the situation. Craig told me he wanted his family back. Craig told me he also wanted to come live with me again. I told him, "It's not up to me. It's up to God now".

Not to mention it wasn't that simple. He had to do what he needed to do to get back. First thing was he had to get the other woman out of our covenant. Our marriage was between God, Craig and me. God was not pleased with me or Craig at the moment either. Every time Craig did something that hurt me, I wanted to get back at him. Somebody had to grow up, though, and I told the Lord it will definitely be me!

I hurried up and dropped Craig off. I felt like the second place chick, so I just knew I had to go! I went home and I still wanted to finish up the conversation Craig and I were having, but he did not answer the phone. I called him twice. I didn't want to seem desperate but at the same time I also felt like I wasn't important to him anymore or good enough. The devil is a liar! I just knew he went with that girl who was blowing his phone up at the restaurant. He had to kiss and make up for not answering the phone for her.

The next morning Craig decided to call me around seven or eight o'clock in the morning. He must have just got dropped off. I didn't say anything because I know how it is to get that last hoorah out of your system. He was trying to get me to come over there, but I told him I could not get myself off course and go chill with him, that would be defeating the purpose of us healing and stopping our growth in the Lord, so no!

Two days later Zayiah and I decided to go to the gym. It was time for me to get back in shape, so Zayiah became my motivator. I loved it! Craig kept calling me while I was headed to the gym. I answered the phone and told him I was about to go to the gym. He didn't believe me, so I video chatted with him when I got there to prove a point.

I hung up the phone and I was ready to put in some work. I worked on cardio and leg strengthening. I got on all the cardio machines at Planet Fitness for 15 minutes each. Then I worked on my legs and stretched for another 30 mins. After I finished my workout, I felt good but sore.

On my way home I was driving and the directions took us a way where we had to pass by the street Craig stayed on. I peeked to see if I could find him doing whatever, and I saw Craig standing in the middle of the street smiling with his hands up. I thought to myself, "Damn, he saw me." Then before the street got out of my view, I saw a black car pull up in front of him. At first I assumed that he was high and that whoever was in the car just didn't want to hit him. But as I thought about that, something wasn't sitting well in my spirit.

I instantly called my daughter and gave her the details of the car. Angel said she had witnessed the mysterious mistress one day when she went to visit Craig at Alicia's house. Angel told me the girl he was talking to also had a black car. When I heard that my face dropped... I hurried up and called Craig's phone. I just kept calling, calling and calling. He didn't answer any of my calls, so I just left him a message. In the message I told him he needed to pick a side and stay there!

I was so angry I couldn't even move. I blocked every contact I had with Craig after that. I knew I was going into a cycle of depression, anger and worry. It got to the point where I didn't know what to do. I was playing music and Zayiah switched the song to "This Is My Exodus," and I broke out in tears. Zay was talking to me, saying that the enemy was tempting me to resort to the old Keonna ways that would hinder what God was doing in me. Eventually I calmed down. I took a bath, prayed and asked God to forgive me if I was overstepping my boundaries. I didn't wanna be God in Greg's life, so I had to leave my hands out of the situation and allow God to be God.

CHAPTER 26
Moment of Reflection

I really think the reason I was with Craig for so long was because he was the only person I'd ever let in on my secret that I had a burn on my forehead. I was so self-conscious I didn't think I was beautiful at all, so when he called me sexy ma, it felt good. He found that out from helping me take my hair out of my braids. My secret was finally exposed early in our relationship. I believe my first mistake was not letting Craig see my burn up front so he could make his decision to stay or to go!

In our relationship Craig did a lot of wrong to me. Craig would look at other women while we were together in public. When Craig and I were home, Craig used to be on Facebook and Instagram in other women's inboxes. I used to go behind him and check the women by telling them, "Get out of his inbox." And trust me I was not pleased about it! I now realize that was my second mistake. I shouldn't have interfered in what could have ended us a long time ago.

I think I stayed so long because I didn't want to face the fact that I would have to showcase my burn to find the one for me. The final mistake was not loving myself! I allowed all of this to happen for twenty years because I didn't love me, nor did I get shown how to love myself. I allowed the enemy to plant seeds into me at an early age to stop me from finding out who I really am in Christ. But that has changed.

I just want to speak to my readers who are going through similar situations. Never allow the enemy to tell you anything about yourself, especially if God didn't say it. First, read in the Bible what God says about you. Let me start you off with Jeremiah 29:11 "For I know the thoughts that I think toward you, saith the LORD, thoughts of peace, and not of evil, to give you an expected end." The Bible also says study to show thyself approved, rightly dividing the truth. In other words, now you have some homework, seek ye first Him and then you will find you.

CHAPTER 27
Wisdom at Funerals

My pastor called me on the phone and asked what the boys and I were doing on Wednesday. I told him they had to work. He asked me what time they had to go to work. I replied, "They work from 4 p.m. to 10 p.m." He said, "Can you get them to the church by 8 o'clock in the morning?" He needed their help to set up for the funeral of one of our church member's children who had passed away.

I had a sudden urge in my spirit and I said, "No problem, do you need me to serve?" My pastor replied,

"Keonna, wouldn't you just be getting off work?" "Yes, I get off at seven," I responded. My pastor told me, "You should go get some rest." I told My pastor, "I don't sleep." Then he said, "I'll leave that up to you." Next morning I got off of work and talked to God in the car. I asked the Holy Spirit to have His way considering what I would wear. I also told Sean and Zay to get ready.

When all of us were ready we headed out. When we got to church, the ushers asked the boys to help with setting up and moving chairs, etc. I was stationed at the table to help with the seating and giving people water bottles. As I was sitting there I saw one of my church members that I hadn't seen in a while. I walked up to her and said, "Hey lady, long time no see." The lady said, "How have you been? I'm so glad you're here. God knows what to do, my nephew loved you! He used to follow you around that church like a puppy!" I asked her, "Who is your nephew?" She replied, "Makell is my nephew."

It still didn't ring a bell to me, so she went in her envelope and pulled out an obituary. As I was looking at the picture of her nephew, my eyes got watery because I was staring at my friend. I couldn't believe what I was doing. I was serving at my friend's funeral who I didn't even know had passed away. I asked her what happened to him and she said it was self-inflicted. I walked away and started to talk to God. I couldn't believe what was going on.

Tears fell from my eyes and pain came in my chest. I know God is in control, but the way I found out was crazy! I'm glad I went to the funeral, God knew to send me. Thank you, Holy Spirit! I couldn't just wipe my tears and let it be done. They brought the casket into the church. The casket was sitting by the front entrance door. I went inside because I didn't want to believe it was true. I looked at the body and he seemed to be at peace. Makell's auntie was in the sanctuary and she saw me crying. She told me to come over and sit by her. She held me while I was crying and she told me to let it out.

As I was crying I burst out laughing. I said out loud, "I bet you Makell had something to do with this. I bet you Makell asked God, "Can you please let her be at my funeral?" I really didn't know Makell loved the idea of me. I had just left Craig at the time, so I was open to a new thing. Makell was a little young, but age ain't nothing but a number. He was tall, handsome and had a smile that would light up a room. We never got the chance to really go out on a date or interact other than at church.

The funeral was an open casket and while I was looking at his face, I noticed that the side of his face was so packed with makeup. There was hairspray to make it look like a shape up. I'm assuming that he killed himself with a gun, and that hurt my heart because you don't know what people go through. You never know what's behind people's smiles. I started feeling like if I hadn't listened to my pastor, I could have done something that would have changed the situation.

When I first met him, one of the members saw me smile at him. She saw us flirting, basically and she pulled me to the side and said, "I wouldn't go there if I were you, trust me," so I left it alone. I just was thinking if I had not left it alone would he still be here? I know I'm a very good influencer. I'm doing the right thing, glory to God, so something to me is just saying I could've done something.

So I'm learning from my mistakes, and a mistake is, Don't allow anyone else to advise you on what to do if you think you were on good ground. Not taking anything from my church member because I truly believe that she meant well. I just can't help the way I feel. I know I feel like I can help everybody. I know I feel like there's always some good in everyone, but Zay talked to me and told me, "Don't condemn yourself. Everything happens for a reason, and I know all things work for good for them that love the Lord and the Lord will get all the glory after this. Hallelujah, amen!

We received instructions on what to do at the funeral because it was about to start. We had to go behind the casket and when they carried the casket outside, we had to carry the flowers and place them in front of the casket. I was anticipating the word and what God had in store for his people.

It was basically about getting others to the Promised Land. Pastor asked if there was anyone who needed to be saved. He told them to close their eyes and whoever wanted to be saved should raise their hand and he would pray for them right there. I believe three people raised their hands. How many of you know that when people accept salvation and believe in Jesus Christ, heaven rejoices – even when just one soul is saved, and God received three souls that day!

During the service Pastor said, "Let's give God a praise clap," but the audience didn't seem enthused about praising Jesus. People were barely putting their hands together, but when the pastor said, "Let's give Makell a praise clap," the audience gave a standing ovation. I'm nobody's judge, but I really think they had it backwards. God is the creator of this earth. God sent His Son Jesus to die for our sins so that we may have everlasting life with Him in heaven. Jesus paid the price for us.

I just thank God that I was a witness to that moment. Never in a million years would I think that people would give a standing ovation for man but not Jesus. Wow! Thank you, Lord, for saving me and my family. Father God, please forgive those who curse you. Forgive those who clap for their friends and family, and they don't even know that You are everything and much more important than a mere mortal. Lord, you are our Father and our provider. He is our friend, our beginning, our middle, our end. God is our everything!

Lord, please forgive them for not knowing what they do!

CHAPTER 28
Here We Go Again...

I had to call Crag, but I used my daughter's phone to do it. I hadn't spoken with him in a long time, and I didn't want him to think anything by unblocking his number and calling him from my phone. When he answered the phone I said, "Hello?" But he thought it was Angel because he said, "Hey, Angel." I said, "So you don't know my voice no more, huh?" He replied, "I thought it was Angel because it was her number. I don't know why you ain't calling from your phone. Did you block me? Aww man, you blocked it."

I told him the reason I was calling him was because Sean would be graduating soon, and I wanted to know if he was gonna be there. Craig responded, "Why wouldn't I want to come!" I wanted to say, *Maybe because you don't call them or spend time with them.* I kept my mouth shut though. That would have been another conversation that would lead to nowhere. I also asked him what was the name of the store I got my bed from. He said he didn't remember, but I think he was being spiteful. I got off the phone with him and went on with my day. I went out to get my nails done and get something to eat.

After I was done pampering myself, I went home to get ready for work and do Bible study for my family. Having Bible study as a family is quite interesting. The Book of Genesis is something else! God was allowing my family and me to understand more of what was going on during that time. From learning about Adam and Eve to Cain and Abel we were having very interactive conversations. We were reading about how God created the earth in 6 days and rested on the 7th day. We talked about how that was relevant to our sabbath day.

We looked it up, but we didn't get anywhere from that. Then we tried to put the actual days of the week in order. We started questioning ourselves and wondering if Saturday is our Sabbath Day. I can tell you, though, to this day we are still trying to figure that out, LOL. After we were done with our Bible study, we prayed out and I had to be on my way to work. As soon as I got to work I started filling out my paperwork. I got on the phone with Zay, but he really wasn't talking at the moment. I was watching him do push-ups. He knows I like conversation, though, so I ended up hanging up from the call. He texted me back and said that he was about to listen to Thursday night Bible study. I texted him back and said "OK."

When I finished all my paperwork I lay on the couch and a Luther Vandross song popped in my head. It was called, "The One Who Holds My Heart." I started singing the lyrics to the song. Anthony heard me singing and said, "Come on, come on." I knew that meant to play the song.

So I googled it and we started to sing. As I was singing I started looking at pictures of Craig and our family. I came to another realization that Craig really isn't with me or his family anymore. I didn't know what God was doing, but when I heard this song it reminded me that I'd rather have hard times together than to have it easy apart. I'd rather have the one who holds my heart .

But then I thought about Zay and I heard more lyrics play in my head. Then the music in my head paused and for a brief moment I rethought about what was going on. I knew I was not faking anything with Zayiah. My heart just loves people very much. Especially for different things, different ways and I know Craig did a lot of things, but who didn't. I know I was trying to do what was right. Our separation was best for Craig and me.

More importantly I thank God money was never a factor. In any of my relationships it wasn't built on money, it was built on love, true love. I really love having both Craig and Zay. I just thank God because I'm blessed, and I know Craig might be my past. It seems that Isaiah is to be my future. I know I still haven't healed from my relationship because I just cried. I cried so hard that I had to call my daughter. I couldn't think of anybody else I wanted to call, and I don't know if that's sad or not.

I started contemplating in my head going back and forth between Craig and Isaiah. For Craig it was like, man, I've really been with him for a long time and we started something. But on the other hand God was showing me that Isaiah was looking promising as well. I really didn't want to get upset with anyone or make anyone feel upset because of how I felt.

My decisions about my life caught me at a very controversial fork in the road. I called Angel to vent about what I was going through. When Angel answered the phone she asked me, "What's wrong?" I told her I missed Craig and I had just sung a song that reminded me of him. "When that song popped up in my head it brought back memories of my past," I said.

In the middle of me speaking to Angel, she heard Ant in the background asking me what was the matter with me. She took our picture on Facetime. I said, "Ant, you know what's wrong with me, don't you? Who do I miss, Anthony?" "You miss Craig," he said.

In the middle of me talking to Angel, Zay video called my phone. Zay saw something was wrong. He said, "Wourn (his nickname for me)? Are you ok?" I responded, "Yeah, I'm okay." Even me saying that to Zay, I knew I couldn't keep nothing from Zaiyah. He said, "It looks like something is wrong with you." I told him I just got done crying and told him about all I was going through between my love triangle. He asked me if I talked to God about it. I said, "No I didn't," and I started to cry again.

Anthony jumped in the camera and told Zay I missed Greg. It started getting late so we got in our midnight Bible study. We started praying, but I was getting sleepy. The enemy always tries to put me to sleep when I try to get in the Word. Next thing I knew after prayer, morning came. When I got up I did my normal ritual. I got ready to leave and when I did leave I prayed in the car. I talked to God about what happened the night before, and I asked what He has for my life as far as my relationship life is concerned, He would push me to it.

Then a thought clicked in my head: Would God want me to go backwards? Then a second thought came to my head, *I'm not God, and God can do anything!* Then another thought, *Do you want to just give up on your husband?* Too many thoughts came into my head at once. I asked the Lord to please help and deliver me from confusion. "I love them both. Show me how to leave this in Your hands because I can't bear it. It's too heavy! My destination is on the line. Guide me to the right decision. I decree and declare I will finish my course strong and You will be pleased. The Lord will say to me, 'Well done, good and faithful servant,' in the name of Jesus."

CHAPTER 29
My Failed Test

It was a very busy day, I'd just gotten off from working an eight-hour shift overnight. It was 7 in the morning. I did my regular morning ritual, I talked to the Lord in the driveway before I stepped foot into my household. As I was walking to the steps toward my back door, I couldn't wait to see Zayiah and lie down. I was thinking, *Home sweet home. I get to relax a little bit before I do what I have to do.*

Lo and behold, I see a pile of dishes in my sink. I mean it was like Mt. Everest. Personally, I can't stand to see my house out of order. Another hour and a half went to cleaning up the kitchen. My children didn't understand that after a certain time at night the kitchen is closed, especially because they don't clean up after they're done. I felt like I couldn't lie down to get rest knowing my house ain't right. Plus I am the leader and I have to lead by example.

It didn't stop there after I had cleaned the kitchen. I needed a bath and a shower. After I got out and got dressed, I told Zay, "Let's go!" We planned the day before to go to the laundromat. We drove to a laundromat, but I couldn't find parking on the nearby streets. I was not about to get a ticket! We ended up using the GPS to see if there was another laundromat that also included parking. There was one a couple of blocks down the street from our house on Georgia Ave, so we went to another laundromat and did our laundry there.

While the clothes were in the washer, we went to get something to eat at Wendy's. When we got back from getting our eats we ate our food in the parking lot. I went with Isaiah to check the clothes and this lady came to me and asked me a question about my health.

"Are you trying to lose weight the healthy way?" she asked. "Yes," I replied. She said, "God is good! Follow me to my car. I wanna show you some of my nutritional products!"

When I went to her car she had boxes and boxes of green tea packages. There were two green tea packages, one for daytime and one for night. I asked, "Do you take a night time to help your bowel movement?" "Yes, it flushes out everything you ate for the day," she replied. She also gave me a pill for energy and sea moss to try.

Then out of the blue while she went to do her laundry she stopped and asked me a question. She asked, "Is he your son?" "No!" I exclaimed. Again, she asked, "How is he related to you?" I was stuck, I didn't know what to say. "Are you his social worker?" she asked. I burst out laughing because I was trying to figure out for the life of me why she cared. She answered her own questions, I just made subtle, but expressive body movements.

I walked over to Isaiah and told him what she'd said. He said, "You ain't my social worker." I said, "Right! That's what I said." A couple of minutes passed and we were letting the clothes finish the spin cycle. He brought up what had happened earlier in the laundromat. "You know when that lady asked you all those questions, that was a test," he said. "What's the test?" I asked. "The test was to see if you were gonna tell the truth," he replied.

Then I began to think, it was a test! I was so scared to tell the truth about who Zayiah was to me. I was worried about what someone else would think or say. I went to go think about the real matter of the situation. Zayiah put the clothes in the dryer and I went to the car by myself. Again, I asked myself why do I care about what people say? Why couldn't I just tell the truth? I felt like I was doing something wrong because of our age difference.

Then I thought about how I introduced him to a lot of people as my son. The enemy was playing with me. I'd watched him grow up. I cooked for him, I let him stay in the house and he went to school with my kids. Zayiah was older, but he was in the same age group as my kids. He was my son's best friend. They don't even talk to each other anymore because of what God was doing. I can honestly say I didn't do any of this; all I did was pray to God for someone that would treat me right.

I prayed for a man to study with me and to love Christ with me. I felt sorry because I wasn't more specific. I didn't know the person I prayed for would be in my house the whole time. God works in mysterious ways. I'm so tired of trying to please everybody and make sure everyone else is OK. I will not be putting myself on the back burner anymore! It's my time to tell the truth and nothing but the truth and the truth is I love Isaiah. I told him how I honestly felt while I was crying.

I showed Zay the picture I took at the Secret club out in Ocean City with all the people in the background. I told him to imagine all of the men in the picture trying to holla at me. "I still would choose you! I apologize that you have to keep going through this. I'm sorry about denying the truth. I know that God put us together for a greater purpose. I am so sorry that I keep pushing you away. I want you. I can't help that God chose you. All I can do is thank God that it's you.

God allowed you to see how I was getting treated by Greg. That helped from what I see because you know what not to do and how to handle me and that is with care." I love the man God is showing who belongs with me. He tells me I'm beautiful everyday even when I can't find things to say about myself. He is always there to tell me what he sees in me. Praise God! Zayiah loves me for me, even my imperfections. He would say my imperfections are beautiful then kiss my forehead. He has no problem telling me when I'm wrong. I love how he stood on God's word when I questioned it because I didn't want to tell people what was going on. I was tired of hiding it. It was eating me up inside. *Let me just get a divorce already.* Lord, please help me and those who go through insecurities daily.

I hope this message helped someone. My message for me was it is okay, you cannot help who you fall in love with, especially when God is all in it. Also, don't deny what God has blessed and ordained. That's the same thing those Pharisees and religious authorities did to Jesus. Lord, please forgive me. I repent right now in Jesus' name, amen. Hallelujah! All things work for them that love the Lord and are called according to His will!

Encouragement and Reflection

Push, Press and Pray

1. Keep your eye single-focused and fixed on the Lord. Distractions are gonna come, but remember trouble doesn't always last.
2. Always keep God in everything that you do because He always wants you to.
3. Study your Bible. It is the God-given guide while on earth so you can make it into heaven. Remember, not everyone makes it into the pearly gates, some are in hell and others are going to hell when they die (Matthew 7:13-14).

Homework time - Find the red flags in each chapter of this book that could have resulted in a different outcome. If only I had taken the time and seen the red flags at the beginning, I would have had a different life. I'm still grateful for the life I have now.

CHAPTER 30
The Leap

After my date with Greg and all the altercations, I tried to get a good night's rest. That didn't happen because I got a phone call at 12:30 in the morning! It was Greg asking me, "When are we getting a divorce?" I answered him, "I don't have time for this right now. I just got out of the hospital for my shin splints from jumping double Dutch. I need rest!" "Oh... okay," he replied. Then Craig hung up the phone.

The next morning I got up and did some thinking. I decided he was right. It was time to get a divorce. I called Ms. Phil, my spiritual mother, and she told me what I needed to do and where I needed to go. I immediately started assembling my documents like my marriage license and ID. After I got everything I needed, I went to the family court building and got the files for our divorce. There wasn't any hassle getting the forms either. I went in there, told them the business I needed to conduct, did what I needed to do and they got me out of there. Thank God!

As I was reading the divorce forms, I realized it said I had to get someone to serve the papers to Craig, or I could try to give him the papers myself in person. I knew I wasn't gonna have a problem with giving him the papers because he wanted the divorce or at least that's what his mouth said. So when he came to drop off Adrian's game and controller, I decided that was when I would serve him.

While I was serving him the paper, I even pulled out my phone to record, so I could have proof of me serving him. We had a laughing moment when I said, "You wanted it done. Here's your papers." As I handed him his papers, Craig began to smile. I told him, "Just go ahead and have a good life. I hope this makes you happy; that's all I ever wanted." We both had been holding each other back.

After I wished him well it was finally my chance to start my new life! It was time for me to further the process of getting myself aligned with God and what He wants to get done in my life as I relinquish control.

Whatever God has for my life, I want it! Devil, I'm on your neck! I'm coming for everything you tried to take from me! I was a little sad because I never thought I was gonna get a divorce from my husband. I did cry sometimes because Craig's words were not matching up with his actions. I felt like crap and he always used to say to me, "I'm loving only you, forever is where I stand." *I Did Not See Any of That!*

I also felt like I'd lost my best friend. Again, I had been with that man since I was sixteen years old and I'm thirty-six now! I didn't see a fight in him to keep our marriage alive. All I saw was a smile on his face. But *now* it's time for me to smile and move on. Lord, I need you to help me with the grieving process because I cannot handle this on my own.

My mind and emotions are everywhere, but I stand and believe in your word that you will never leave me nor forsake me. Your plans for me are good and not evil. Your plans are to give me hope and a future in Jesus' mighty name. Amen!

Craig, I forgive you for all that you have done to me and the things that we've been through together. The things I allowed to happen and please forgive me for all of the things that I have done to you that were spiteful in retaliation. To hurt you back and to get even. Two wrongs don't make a right. I release myself so you and I can be free. Free to be who God called us to be and be great disciples on the earth. God is calling us higher in Jesus' name. Amen

Well wishes,

A strong resilient woman

CHAPTER 31
Ah Ha!

As I look back I realize the truth was right in front of me the whole time. I had recently gone to church and my pastor was preaching on, "You only pursue things you value. So if you love the Lord you will pursue Him." Then it hit me, a light bulb came on. Thank you, Holy Spirit. I realize now, Craig didn't really love me. Since we have been separated, not once has Craig come to fight for or pursue me. I went back for him twice and the Lord told me not to. I was going in the wrong direction!

I used to get in my car when I was leaving work and look back just to see if he was in the car. My van had a problem with the doors, so he knew how to get in without a key. He has not once hunted for or come to see me. I was hurt. I couldn't believe I had been with this person for twenty-two years and there was no fight in him. I broke down in tears when I got home. This grief is getting to me for sure, but I know in the end God will get all of the glory out of my life.

For the life of me I couldn't figure out why I was having a hard time with that whole situation. I just thank God that He sent a member of my church to help me along this journey. Momma Phil just recently got a divorce from her husband, and she could relate to what I was going through. She asked me if I was okay, and I told her no! Momma Phil replied, "That's the expected, baby. I was there and it was hard, but you will get through it, trust me!"

I just thank God for her. It was good to be able to talk to someone who could relate to what I was going through at the time. Most importantly I knew she would come to comfort me with the spirit of the Lord. You have to be able to discern and know the difference between someone who's in your corner and someone who is just in your business! I just want you guys to know when you're going through life issues... don't smoke it away or drink it away. Nor should you sex it away or try to act like it's non-existent. Trust me, I've been there and gone through all of those phases. Those things don't do anything but mask the problem because it'll still be there at the end of the day.

I even tried to cut my hair off for a new change, but I felt the same. I looked good, but I didn't feel good on the inside. It was pointless. People do so much to the outside appearance to appear happy and at peace. But on the inside they're crying out for healing from heartbreak. They're also crying out from abuse and molestation. How many people can relate to what I'm about to ask: Don't you just want to be loved? Shoot... I know I do. I want to come home and be at peace, not get into petty arguments. I dare you to reflect and talk to the Lord about your problems. As a matter of fact, don't focus on the problems at all, you can acknowledge the problem, but give it to God and finally focus on the problem solver – Jesus.

CHAPTER 32
Finalizing My Divorce

The day had finally arrived, August 23rd. I woke up that morning at 8:29 a.m. I had set an alarm for my divorce hearing. The enemy was trying to stop me from moving forward because neither Craig nor I had our login information. I had gotten an email in regards to my divorce and they told me what time I needed to be on Zoom. I had to quickly call family court to tell them I needed the information to log in.

When I finally got the information, I logged on and called Craig to make sure he was on the call as well.

Nothing but death was gonna stop me from getting my divorce. Can you believe he was asleep! Not today, my man! I asked him, "Did you get an email yet?" "No," he said. "I called and got the information, so get up. I'm about to send it to you. Log on before 9 o'clock," I said.

When we got on the Zoom call the judge asked us to state our name and raise our right hand. The judge asked, "Do you swear to tell the truth, the whole truth and nothing but the truth, so help you God?" We both said I do. I could also hear Craig in the background saying, "Bae, how do you do this?" I couldn't believe what my ears were hearing. I thought he didn't even love her. At least that's what he told me. You know what's crazy? When he needed a place to stay he said anything out of his mouth to convince her. He could've gone to rehab and still been with his family. But as you know things clearly did not work out that way.

The judge asked, "When did you two get married?" "March 29, 2004," I replied. "In what state did you two get married?" the judge asked. I answered, "In the state of Virginia at Saint Brides correctional facility." "Do you have any children together?" the judge asked. I replied, "Yes." The judge asked, "Were any of your children under the age of 18?" "Yes, two of them," I said. "Are you looking for custody child support, or do you have any property together to be disputed?" the judge asked. "No, not at this time," I responded. "Well I am going to grant you, the plaintiff, a full divorce. I am going to sign it today, but you have 30 days to change your mind. It will be sent to the address that we have on file. Thank you for your time. You both have a good day," the judge said.

I replied, "Thank you so much. God bless you." We both got off the phone and I wanted to call him so bad to say, "We did it! Now it's time for us to start our new lives and just be happy." As much as I wanted to do it, I didn't. I didn't want to entertain anything else now that I finally had my divorce. All I was waiting on was the ink to dry and the paperwork to come in the mail. Emotions started to rise because I'd been with Craig for 21 years and I was finally free!

All of the things that we'd been through together, the good, bad and the ugly, it didn't kill us, it made us strong individuals who gained a lot of wisdom along the way. I was closer to his side of the family, so I couldn't really talk to my siblings. I didn't really talk to my siblings like that anyway, so I always felt alone, especially when I was going through it with Craig. I felt like I pushed everyone I had away because of the relationship I had with Craig. I couldn't do anything that I wanted to do because of what he would think or say. I kept allowing Craig to use my past every time we got in an argument so he could get his way.

He used to say I was a slut and that I was lying when I told him I got raped. When I wanted to visit Sherrice he also said I just wanted to go out to Baltimore to have sex with guys. That was his way of getting me to stay to prove him wrong and show that I was about him. He was just playing reverse psychology on me. We did absolutely nothing but argue some more or look at television.

I'm finally free, today is a new day to figure out who Keonna really is. Scripture says in 2 Corinthians 5:17, "Therefore if any man be in Christ he is a new creature: behold old things are passed away; behold all things become new." God called me friend! Eventually, you will realize that no matter how good you are to a person it won't make them good to you or for you. I have finally realized I cannot change him, I can only pray for him. I have been taught through the Holy Spirit, love does not hurt. Scripture says in 1 Corinthians 13:4-5, "Love is patient, love is kind. It does not envy, it does not boast, it's not proud. It does not dishonor others, It is not self-seeking, it is not easily angered, it keeps no record of wrongs." Whoever lives in love lives in God, and God in them. The beautiful thing about life is that when you wake up, it's a brand new day. God gives us grace to start over and change, you can grow from what you have been through and you aren't defined by your mistakes. It ain't over until God says it's over! So please allow me to reintroduce myself...

CHAPTER 33
In the Midst of the Storm

My pastor once told me, "Why tell a lie when the truth will do?" When I heard my pastor say that it made perfect sense to me. Why tell a lie that causes trouble and makes you tell more lies? No one can point the finger at you or expose you about your own truth if you confess it first. In the Bible we have a great example. Jesus never lied, he was the perfect one. He was verbally attacked and lied on for being the truth and telling about it.

It was a great morning. In the middle of the night I got up out of bed and went downstairs to the living room where God told me to meet Him. I talked with Him for a little while, I felt like it was a new beginning to our relationship with each other. After I was done talking with Him I dozed off on the couch. Later on when the sun came up, Isaiah woke me up looking for me. He asked me, "Are you okay?" I told him, "Yes, I was talking to God."

After that I got up and went upstairs to get ready for church. Isaiah told Alexa to play the song "Optimistic" and we began to dance. He was trying to get me out of my slump because the night before I had to go to a lounge to promote my cousin's business. My cousin started a Double Dutche business, which is a double Dutch team that teaches youth how to jump rope. We not only teach them how to jump rope, but we prepare them for professional competitions.

The host that got us to come to the lounge asked if we could bring the rope to jump. It wasn't busy there, it was a light crowd. There were only 15 people there including us, but we made the most of it. I couldn't believe they had us jumping in a lounge. We were the first that ever did it; I'm sure of it. I also read an article before going to the lounge that night that one of my pastors gave me and God was speaking through the article.

The article basically said take Jesus everywhere with you, give Jesus the key to every door of your heart and let him clean it up. I had thought going to a lounge would be a form of compromise for a job, but that article blessed me and told me if I had Jesus with me and was obedient, then I would be at peace with the Prince of peace.

After we finished dancing we woke the house up and got dressed. Everyone headed to the car, but we noticed my oldest son was there and he hadn't been going to church lately. I talked to him prior and said stop running from God and run to him because He is the one that can change all the things going wrong in his life. So I called his phone and told him to come outside so we wouldn't be late.

Mind you, everyone in the house knows the time we wake up and leave for church, which is 10:15 a.m., but if they are running a little behind they have until 10:30

at the most. While I was on the phone with him he said, "I'm putting my shoes on." "Hurry up, Damonte! You already know the time we leave," I said. He didn't respond so I hung up. We got in the car at 10:30, but I waited 10 more minutes and I got upset. I said out loud, "He's getting left, I'm about to pull off. God ain't tell me to wait, He said go!"

All he had to do was say he wasn't going, but get out of my house if you're not going to church. As for me and my house we will serve the Lord! I pulled off and I had to fly to church. See, the enemy has been testing me since the night before. I was still thinking about the whole situation on the way to church, but Isaiah DJ'd and turned on some gospel music to ease me.

I told Isaiah to text Damonte and tell him, "Don't bring nobody in my house. Lock up the house and leave." Isaiah texted Damonte through his phone instead of mine. Damonte replied, "I got work, not worried about anything else, but my daughter's birthday is in a couple of days." I couldn't keep entertaining Damonte, so I was pretty much done with it. The whole mission today was to go to church and tell the pastor that God told us to shift. When I got to the church I entered right into a

Holy Ghost-filled worship service. I was at ease because by the time I got there I hadn't missed anything.

The worship service did more than calm me down, it brought my peace back because in that moment everything else faded away. I was giving God His glory and praise. The pastor spoke a great message, God gave us a lot of confirmation, wisdom and preparation, especially since we were getting ready to talk to the pastor about shifting to another church. The moral of what I heard God say today was when God tells you to move, you are supposed to move!

I am glad the pastor said that; it was like God was giving me confirmation about speaking to the pastor about what's taking place, which was a big transition. I was excited about where God was taking me and my family. I felt a way because I'd been with that church for 10 years plus. The way I felt when I left my husband whom I'd been with for 21 years was the same way I was feeling about leaving the church.

Everything was hitting me at once. I was honored that God chose me, but I knew I had to be prepared, as to whom much is given much is required. We went to talk to the pastor briefly in a private room and he agreed that we needed to be obedient to God and do what He said to do. After he talked to us, he prayed with us. He told us he loved us and left.

We decided to go to my dad's house because Sean needed to check on his moped. We ate my dad's snacks and food, then we headed back home to get rest. While we were in the car we were talking about Damonte saying he didn't go to church because he was only worried about his daughter. Not to boast or anything, but I did so much for my grand baby and my family and I got an invite to her first birthday party at Chuck E. Cheese. I said I wasn't going and Sean said in a judgmental way, "How you not going to go to your granddaughter's birthday because of her father?"

When he said that I told him I'm not, not going because of her father, I'm not going because of her mother's family. I don't wanna be in a place that makes me feel uncomfortable. When Sean said that, it was like he was trying to shame me. I got the revelation that people will look at the one thing you didn't do instead of everything else you did. I turned the whole music down and I told them that statement. I told them that's why I follow God because He doesn't judge me that way. Sean started back talking and speaking disrespectfully to me and I pulled over the car immediately. I got out of the car and opened his door and told him, "Get the f**k out my car and walk home! You're moving out of the room and going downstairs in the basement where disrespectful people go." He got out and yelled, "I don't care!" still running that mouth. I'm surprised I didn't pop him in it.

When we pulled up to the house we saw Deonte's moped outside. That meant he lied about work, didn't leave my house and when I came in the backyard he had the basement door wide open. I went in the door while he was walking out and I said, "Why did you lie and say you had work, but ain't never go?" He replied, "What are you talking about? I just got back and had to get some oil for my moped." I knew he was lying through his teeth because the moped looked like it hadn't been moved since we left.

I told him, "Your brother's out there walking because he wanted to be disrespectful, following you! You are not even being the example. You are supposed to be the big brother and tell him, 'Don't be talking to Mom like that. That's wack!'" He jumped off topic and said, "Isaiah's wack!" I asked him, "How's Isaiah wack? Ain't he following Christ?" He yelled back, "You're dating a 20 year old." I said, "So... ain't nothing wrong with that. And I'mma keep doing it."

That was a truth reveal. Damonte had still been feeling salty and holding a grudge about Isaiah and me I kind of knew deep down. He'd started to bring different friends around and give Isaiah the silent treatment. Damonte doesn't call or check on me, sometimes he's in the same room and won't speak to me unless I say something.

I really just hope while I'm still here on this earth that I can have a relationship with my son whom I love very much. The crazy thing about this is before Isaiah and I started to get serious I told Damonte, "I will leave Isaiah alone if y'all gonna be friends. I don't want you to lose your friend."

I felt so bad I started questioning God about what was going on, "God, are you sure Isaiah is the one for me?" I've pushed Isaiah away so many times just to make sure this is ordained. Yes, I thought about the age difference, but most importantly, I thought about his friendships, not with just Deonte but with my other children as well. I was willing to risk my love with Zay for someone that doesn't even bother to say, Hey Mom, do you need anything today or can I help around the house?

I think my son wanted me to stay with his father for the rest of my life and be miserable. I hope he understands one day that I just want to be loved right, happy, appreciated, respected and with someone who's after God's heart. That was my prayer. I'm not apologizing anymore. I could not change what I prayed so Damonte went away on his moped. Angel, Isaiah and I went in the house and went on about our day.

Isaiah and I went upstairs and cleared Deandre's room out and put his stuff in the hallway. I had to get my mind off what just happened, so Zay and I prayed to The One that I know can change all things. After prayer Zay said, "Let's go throw the football around." I said, "Cool, let me ask Angel if she wants to come." On my way to ask Angel she was coming up the stairs. She asked, "Did one of y'all up here leave the front door

263

wide open?" I said, "I don't know. Probably Sean once he realized he messed up. He probably came home and saw his belongings in the hallway. But I tell you what, if he leaves my house open like that again, he will have to find somewhere else to live because it won't be here." Angel replied, "I wanna go throw the ball around!" So we locked the house up and left again.

Zay couldn't find the ball. He thought he left it over my dad's house so we stopped by Walmart to get another football. Playing football did the trick for a minute to clear my mind of what was going on at the time. We went to the park, but we were done playing catch with that slippery ball in 20 minutes and were out! We headed back home with no sign of Sean or Damonte.

I asked Isaiah to get the food out of the car that somebody gave us from church. He went to get the food and saw the other football he said he forgot right in his face. Sometimes he doesn't look for anything right, it is right in his face when he looks. I know Sean had to get his moped fixed up, so I was trying to let him be responsible. It was getting late, so I told Angel and Zay to check on him for me to make sure he was safe. Isaiah called him and Deandre said he was on his way. It made me feel good to know that our dispute didn't divide the family.

Isaiah texted him and told him he wanted to talk with him when he got here. When Sean got here Isaiah left and spoke to him, I don't know exactly what happened but Sean was putting his stuff back in his room. I let that whole situation rest for the night and I watched a movie. Scripture says in Ephesians 6:1-4, "Children, obey your parents in the Lord, for this is right. Honor your father and mother (this is the first commandment with a promise), that it may go well with you and that you may live long in the land. Fathers, do not provoke your children to anger, but bring them up in the discipline and instruction of the Lord."

CHAPTER 34
The Wake Up

My auntie Carolyn messaged me on Facebook and said, Hi, can you call your friend and give her some encouraging words because we are going to court tomorrow. God promised me that my children are going to be alright. I have faith and I'm not worried. God's word is true. She has faith too but she's just a little scared. Don't let her know I talked to you. Please do it for me. Thank you. I couldn't call her back right away because I was busy with helping the youth learn how to jump. As soon as I got home I got right on it. I called her back but she didn't answer, so I just prayed for her. The next morning Tiesh returned my call and whispered to me on the phone that she was in court. She said, "I don't know if you are some kind of entity for God, but today is my court date, so can you pray with me?" I didn't tell my bestie that her mother had called me. I just left it alone and was obedient and prayed. I prayed for my friend, not only her but the jury and the judge. I was hoping for a call to make sure she was good after court, but she didn't call me and I did not want to overstep my boundaries. The next day I saw her like a post on my page on Instagram so I figured everything worked out in glory to God.

I got a phone call from my brother days later asking, "Did ma call you?" I said, "No, why?" He replied, "Your best friend and her brother got 37 years in jail each for the death of her husband."

My face dropped because my bestie had just liked a post on my page. Everything happens for a reason. I know God's thoughts are not my thoughts and His ways are not my ways. Everything He does is just and right. I just hope that His will is being done in the midst of it all. Wow, it really hit me. My best friend just got sentenced 37 years and she has five children under the age of eighteen.

I sat down to reflect on the things that had transpired in my life. What if I had decided to call a hit on Craig? Or what if I had taken matters into my own hands to harm him? Would it be the right thing or the wrong thing? Obviously the wrong thing, if it would've done more harm than good. I would have taken a life from the earth and God said, "Thou shalt not kill." He also said forgive and love your enemies. It's easier said than done, but all are capable of doing it.

If I acted in such a manner as to kill or get revenge, I probably would have ended up in prison or a casket. I just thank God I made the decision to call on His Son Jesus and not a person... In life when we are going through abusive relationships, we tend to call family for help instead of God. We should use the wisdom to call the police and in most cases some are too afraid to tell anyone. They are afraid of judgment or afraid to leave the person they are with. Some people are one turn from making the wrong decision and we don't see it coming.

CHAPTER 35
It's Almost Christmas

It was the middle of December and I still had a lot going on in my life. I was trying to still keep up with my double Dutch and get my cleaning service off the ground and that's not even a speck of all I was going through. Isaiah and I had to work very hard when it came to the cleaning service. We'd been using an app called Handy to get clients, which also means we had to do the jobs first in order to get paid and get the clients. The pay was very little. For instance, we would accept a job to clean a house with 3 bedrooms and 3 bathrooms, but they would pay us $70.

It's really an investment to get clients not just the money, but boy we did a lot of work with little pay. I say this affirmation out loud every day: "If a man doesn't work he doesn't eat. I will plan my work and work my plan. I will work only legal jobs and not illegal ones, in Jesus' name, amen." I had to keep saying that so I could manifest motivation into myself.

I went to church one Sunday and after service one of the church members asked me if I would be interested in participating in a Christmas play. She said God told her to ask if Isaiah and I would like to join them. With no hesitation I said, "Yes," and she told us which parts we would be playing. I was playing Eve and Isaiah was Adam. God showed he had a sense of humor with that.

We only had three weeks to practice and in that duration we probably only practiced 4 times. Of course we had to memorize our lines, but we were also dancing. Now with all that we were going through, if we wanted to nail our performance, we had to make time for us to practice in the house by ourselves. It was getting closer to the deadline of the play, and before I knew it Friday had arrived. It was the last practice at the church with everyone, but it was really the first practice with everyone.

When we arrived at the church we thought we were late, but we were the only ones there except for our Pastor Tee. We made some small talk and just like that she asked the hard hitting question. "What's going on with you two? When are y'all getting married?" she said. "We wanted to wait to get the rings and the wedding situated so we can do it all at once," Isaiah answered.

When I tell y'all the spirit started speaking through our pastor, I mean it couldn't have been clearer than a window. "You guys want to make sure you are in a good position with God. You oughta go to the J and P (Justice of Peace) to get y'all's marriage license so you can be right in the sight of God," Pastor Tee said.

I looked at Isaiah and told him, "You know God placed us here. Look around, we are the only ones here and Pastor Tee had a message for us. We just got the okay from God to get married." "Right! We're going on Monday! It's not about the wedding or the rings, it's about doing what's right in the eyes of God," Zayiah said. Isaiah started getting all the information together. He searched for what we needed to have before we went to the court building. After Pastor Tee was done talking to us, we got some pizza and continued with our practice. It feels so good to know that God is ordering our steps to let us know that we are in good standing with Him.

First thing Monday morning we went to the court building. We found a parking spot close to the building, which is really difficult by the way. We walked in the court building and they checked our temperature. We walked through the metal detectors and off we went to get our marriage license. I got so excited I wanted to take some pictures to commemorate what was happening. "You aren't allowed to take pictures here," the clerk said. "Oh sorry. I didn't know," I replied.

In my head I was like, *It's really happening.* I had my own thoughts about how my wedding would be if we went. But, who am I kidding? God is in control. I'm just glad I got the right man this go round. Turns out for both parties we just needed our IDs and to not be married to anyone else at the time. We filled out the document with our information and we got it stamped in a matter of seconds. Shoot, they even said we could marry ourselves. I didn't know that was a thing! I didn't want to do it that way. it would've taken the joy out of having someone else doing it and witnessing that very moment.

After we got the license, we agreed to go look at some rings. We found the most amazing rings. It was like God had rings there waiting for us with our names on them. They weren't a set, but they matched. We just needed to get them sized to the right fit for our fingers. Zay immediately started working to get the money to pay for the rings.

It was finally Christmas Day! Isaiah and I were the only ones up and it was 7 a.m. We started telling Jesus, "Happy Birthday" in prayer and Zayiah asked me, "Do you think they are having a birthday party in Heaven right now?" "They should! It is His birthday," I answered.

Zay escorted me downstairs in front of the tree. He started staring me down and gave me that look of excitement and said, "Honey Bun, you mean a lot to me." He got down on one knee, went into the pocket of his robe and pulled out the ring we picked from the pawn shop.

"Honey Bun, I am ready to spend the rest of my life with you and treat you like the Queen you are. From the moment God started showing us we were supposed to be together and every day we spent together getting to know one another it only made us inseparable. I love you so much because you let God use you to show me what I am worth. When God showed me you, he showed me myself. He showed me you are the one for me that I can love, hold and cherish for the rest of my life. I want to know, will marry me?"

I was smiling from ear to ear. I said. "Yes! I will marry you!" Then we shared a big hug and kiss. We also shared the news with my children and Nu took our pictures. Let's just say itt was a Christmas to remember. We exchanged our gifts and sang, "Happy Birthday to Jesus. To be continued...

CHAPTER 36
Had a Dream

The pressure was on! Two out of the seven days leading up to my wedding I hadn't gotten any sleep. I'd been trying to get a wedding cake, a wedding dress with shoes and other wedding accessories. I put my foot down, and I took two Benadryls so I could go to sleep. The night I finally got some rest I had an insanely vivid dream. It felt so real.

I remember that two guys wanted me so they could study the Bible and get the word or at least that's what they approached me about. Of course because of my heart I agreed, and I followed them into their apartment building while I was carrying my Bible. After we got in their apartment, I ushered all of us to begin praying. Instead of them praying with me, they snatched my Bible from me and slammed it on the table. From that moment I realized I was in trouble.

They didn't say it out loud, but I felt that they wanted to rape me. I bumped into the door with my shoulder and it opened. I tried to make a break for it, but when I got to the second door of the building to leave, it was locked. I don't know how, but the door became welded with a nail from the outside. When I tell y'all I called on the name of the Lord, I did it like never before.

I asked God to save me then suddenly the shoes that I was wearing became steel toe and heavy. I kicked the door to create a gap, and then I pressed my shoulder on the door to pop it open. When I opened the door I found myself on a balcony with my dog Mooky. Mooky was wearing an army fatigue coat and she had made a pile of poop in the grass, but it was crazy because we were up very high so she was in what seemed to be a dog area where she could poop.

I looked over the balcony but then I saw that there was a cliff, so I was hesitant to jump. I had to make a decision to let them rape me or jump and figure out if I would still be alive to tell my story. I took my chances and grabbed Mooky tail hook from her coat and it was incredibly stretchable. Mooky didn't budge either because she was like a weight or anchor. I was gliding through the air going down the cliff.

The guys who were trying to get me jumped off the balcony, too, but they were tumbling down the cliff. I got to the bottom around the same time they did, but they didn't see me. Then from out of nowhere a train appeared with rails on the outside and it was able to block the view of the guys from seeing me. I got on the rails and I didn't let go until I knew I was in the clear.

Here is the lesson and moral of the dream: No matter what I've been through in life, God was always there. I was gullible to have done the things I did in the past, whether it was because of my heart or the circumstances I was under. Even before I knew to call on God, He still made a way. Now that I know who God is, I call on Him and He rescues me from danger. What He did for Daniel in the lion's den and Noah in the whale, is the same thing He did for me in that dream and in my life. Even when we don't see a way, God always makes a way.

THE FINAL CHAPTER
True Love Story

It was finally the day of our wedding! I didn't tell a lot of people because some of the ones that I did let in on our happiness, who I thought would give their blessing, fooled me. So we decided that we wouldn't tell any more people, so they couldn't give their input on what God already said. Yes and amen, too. We prayed and asked God to remove any and everybody who didn't belong at our wedding because we didn't want to have any negative spirits with us.

We had been fasting for the past week because we wanted to honor God in the best way possible. So, on the morning of my wedding we read some scriptures about matrimony togetherness. For example, scriptures like 1 Corinthians 13, Ephesians 5, Ecclesiastes 4 and Genesis 2. After we were done reading, Zay and I put on our casual clothes and went to church.

The word comes before anything else. If you know me you know how important my relationship with God is and my walk with Him! We usually do Sunday school before church and it's study time and a little extra breakdown of the word. You guys really should find a good Bible based church to join and get your spirit fed correctly. Anyway, an hour later we began the service.

I'm in the choir and I was starting to remember the songs, so I could give my gift back to God. I am a worshiper, so I lifted Him up extra that day for the many blessings I had already received,and Isaiah is the best one. I'm so grateful and honored to be his future and forever.

During the service after our praise and worship, our bishop let us know what time we would be excused to put our wedding outfits on. I was talking to our drummer girl. The First Lady sent her my way and she asked me if I needed help with anything. It was drizzling out, and I didn't want to get my dress wet. The good thing about rain is its symbols change. In this case it rained all day and our lives changed for the better.

Bishop excused Zay and I early. We got dressed and I prevented Zay from seeing me with my full dress and everything on. I went downstairs to sit while the church prepared for me to walk through. My cousin came to support and she brought her daughter. I gotta tell you it was nothing but God because we didn't have a flower girl and it's not a coincidence that my cousin had some flowers for us.

The church also provided a basket for the rose petals. The most important thing to me about this wedding was the photographer. The photographer at my wedding with Craig was absolutely horrible. He got the wrong pictures of people, didn't take any pictures of my children or my family. God is amazing because two days prior to my wedding I told my first lady that I didn't have a photographer. She said she couldn't make any promises, but she'd see what she could do.

Glory to God because the photographer came through. The flower girl was up first and she did an amazing job with spreading and throwing the petals down. After the flower girl was done I was up next. My walk down song was by Major and it was called, "Why I Love You." I did a praise dance for God and Zay. Trust me, I was going through anxiety from lack of sleep. After Zay would fall asleep I would stay up half of the night to practice the dance routine. Zay used to wake up when I was studying the lyrics and tell me to get some rest. When I came up to the Bishop and Zay I couldn't stop smiling nor could Zay. Zay said, "You look amazing." The Bishop acknowledged our family and friends who came to support us and be our witnesses. Zay's brother was the ring bearer and Angel was the bouquet holder. My oldest son wasn't there, but my other two sons were. My prayer to God excluded my son from being there. Just because he is my son doesn't mean I should compromise. Not to mention the fact that he didn't want to be there.

As we put the rings on each other's hand we repeated after our bishop when we said our vows. Bishop asked, "Is there any man or woman that disagrees with this union? Let them speak now or forever hold their peace." The church went completely silent and I lifted my hand while my other hand was holding Zay's. Bishop said, "You may salute your bride," and Zay saluted me with both hands and at the same time. The church filled with laughter and we shared a kiss.

We walked down the middle aisle as the photographer took more pictures. After we'd been officially married, a lot of our church family and friends wanted to take pictures. Our church family is so amazing and sweet, they blessed and gifted us with cards and a basket. Majority of the cards had money and that was a huge blessing because during service my first lady preached about the double-fold blessings for shame and toil.

Zay and I worked really hard to make our wedding memorable. But God made plenty of ways. He did more than restore our financial situation. He prevented the negative Nancies from coming. God made sure we felt loved by everyone who was there. My favorite part was when Zay's granny came over to me with tears in her eyes. I'd never met her before, but when I saw tears come down her face some almost came down mine as well.

Before I met her, though, I heard a conversation between her and Isaiah. She told him to wait a little longer until he was 21 because if we didn't, that would be statutory rape. But we had already gotten our marriage license and nobody knew that at the time. If it was wrong for us to get married, then we wouldn't have been able to get the license in the first place. She said a little bit more on the phone, but I can't remember what was said. At least for a fact I know that God made some believers that day.

Have mercy on me, O God,because of your unfailing love.

Because of your great compassion,blot out the stain of my sins.Wash me clean from my guilt.

Purify me from my sin.

For I recognize my rebellion;

It haunts me day and night.

Against you, and you alone, have I sinned;

I have done what is evil in your sight.

You will be proved right in what you say,

and your judgment against me is just.

For I was born a sinner—

Yes, from the moment my mother conceived me.

But you desire honesty from the womb,

teaching me wisdom even there.

Purify me from my sins, and I will be clean;

wash me, and I will be whiter than snow.

Oh, give me back my joy again;

you have broken me—

Now let me rejoice.

Don't keep looking at my sins.

Remove the stain of my guilt.

Create in me a clean heart, O God.

Renew a loyal spirit within me.

Do not banish me from your presence,

and don't take your Holy Spirit from me.

Restore to me the joy of your salvation,

and make me willing to obey you.

Then I will teach your ways to rebels,

and they will return to you.

Forgive me for shedding blood, O God who saves;

then I will joyfully sing of your forgiveness.

Unseal my lips, O Lord,

that my mouth may praise you.

You do not desire a sacrifice, or I would offer one.

You do not want a burnt offering.

The sacrifice you desire is a broken spirit.

You will not reject a broken and repentant heart, O God.

Look with favor on Zion and help her;

rebuild the walls of Jerusalem.

Then you will be pleased with sacrifices offered in the right spirit—

with burnt offerings and whole burnt offerings.

Then bulls will again be sacrificed on your altar.

Just know it ain't over until God says it's OVER!

About The Author

Keonna Brock-Smith is a servant of God who has known difficult times in her life. Those difficulties have not made her bitter, though, because she has had God to see her through every step of the way. She wrote this book to motivate people to live for God.

One of her hobbies is jumping double Dutch. She is a coach for JumpDC where she teaches youth how to jump double Dutch, which helps to lift their spirits. She is a member of Faith Assembly of Christ, Inc., where she is a praise dancer and she sings in the choir.

Keonna is a loving wife and mother of four and grandmother to one. She lives in the Washington, DC area. This is her first book and she plans to write more in the future.